INTEGRAL YOGA

Originated by the great Indian sage Sri Aurobindo, Integral Yoga has been presented in this volume by Dr. Haridas Chaudhuri in the context of contemporary western thinking. It expounds the concept of harmonious and creative living on the basis of a fruitful reconciliation of the self-perfecting mysticism of the East and the rationalistic humanism of the modern West. It gives a dynamic form, an evolutionary perspective, and a creative impetus to the ancient mystic idea of union with the Eternal. In his Foreword to the book, Dr. Pitirim A. Sorokin of Harvard University has called it "the best one-volume work on this subject."

Dr. Chaudhuri is Professor of Philosophy and President of the California Institute of Asian Studies in San Francisco. He also serves as President of the Cultural Integration Fellowship, a group dedicated to the promotion of cultural understanding between East and West. He received his doctorate in philosophy from the University of Calcutta in 1947 and, before coming to the United States at the invitation of Dr. Frederic Spiegelberg of Stanford University, he was a member of the educational service of the government of West Bengal and Chairman of the Department of Philosophy at Krishnagar College. His books on meditation and yoga reveal him not only as an eminent exponent of the spirit of Indian culture but also as an original thinker of deep spiritual insight.

INTEGRAL YOGA

The Concept of Harmonious and Creative Living

BY

HARIDAS CHAUDHURI

Professor of Philosophy and Chairman of the Department of South Asia, American Academy of Asian Studies, San Francisco; and President, Cultural Integration Fellowship

WITH A FOREWORD BY PITIRIM A. SOROKIN

Professor of Sociology and Director of The Research Center in Creative Altruism Harvard University

A QUEST BOOK

Published under a grant from the Kern Foundation

THE THEOSOPHICAL PUBLISHING HOUSE
Wheaton, Ill., U.S.A.
Madras, India / London, England

First Published in 1965
Second Impression 1970

First U.S.A. edition 1974

Published by The Theosophical Publishing House, Wheaton, Illinois, a department of The Theosophical Society in America, by arrangement with George Allen & Unwin Ltd., London.

Chaudhuri, Haridas.
Integral yoga.

(A Quest book)
Includes bibliographical references.
1. Yoga. I. Title.
B132.Y6C58 1974 181'.45 73-17170
ISBN 0-8356-0444-6

PRINTED IN THE UNITED STATES OF AMERICA

TO MARY CALKINS BROOKE

Whose one dream of life was
To see all discords dissolve in love

FOREWORD

In my humble opinion the *Integral Yoga* by Haridas Chaudhuri is the best one-volume work on this topic. His analysis of the integral yoga, its principles and its relationship to other forms of yoga, to modern Western thought, to different systems of philosophy and religion including mysticism, is so admirably done that there is no need for a lengthy preface on my part.

Instead I can whole-heartedly recommend the book to all who are interested in yoga and, more generally, in the basic philosophical, religious and moral problems of man. Integral yoga suggests its own solutions to many of these perennial quests. For the Western psychologists, psychiatrists, educators and moral leaders particularly significant are: Chapters II–V in which the important differences of the integral yoga from the ancient religious and mystical traditions are clearly shown, and Chapters VII and VIII which outline the methods and techniques of the integral yoga used for the transformation of human personality.

PITIRIM A. SOROKIN
Director, Research Center in Creative Altruism, Harvard University

CONTENTS

CONTENTS

INTRODUCTION

PASSION for diversity-in-unity is a central characteristic of India culture. It has resulted in an appreciation of divergent viewpoints in the light of some underlying principle of unity.

In Hindu philosophy Truth is affirmed to be one and universal, and at the same time endowed with endless forms and modes of expression. Being is affirmed to be nondual, but at the same time multi-form and multi-dimensional. The destiny of life is affirmed to be the same, namely, union with the eternal, but it is believed that there are many ways leading to the same destination.

It is this nondualistic outlook which has produced an amazing spirit of toleration and comprehensive understanding in Indian thought. The great religions of the world are accepted as different avenues of approach to the common goal of integration with ultimate reality. The great founders of world religions are accepted as equally divine manifestations in history of the same dynamic world-spirit. The different philosophies of the world are viewed as various modes of intellectual formulation of that concrete fullness of existence which is essentially non-verbal and non-intellectual. Different political ideologies are perceived as relatively valid means of self-development of different countries and nations.

Over the centuries all manner of experiments have been made in India with the spiritual truth, that is to say, in the field of living in harmony with the Supreme Being. The findings of such experiments are embodied in her traditional yoga systems. It is believed that different yoga systems are particularly suitable for different individuals who belong to different psychological types. But in essential design they are all attuned to the same goal, namely, direct union with the ultimate ground of existence.

This concept of union with the ground of existence—the concept of yoga—is pivotal to India culture. All religious movements are oriented to it. All philosophical tendencies spring from it. Even social and political ideologies have to reckon with it. The task of social reconstruction and political rebuilding must be in keeping with man's ultimate spiritual destiny, to wit, union with the Supreme Being.

Man's direct union with the ultimate ground of existence may briefly be described as existential union. The essence of yoga is existential union. During the Middle Ages, negative and static elements in the concept of existential union were specially emphasized. It was believed by many that in order fully to realize the supreme truth one has sooner or later to renounce the world of social action (*saṁsāra*). After a person attains spiritual integration, all his springs of action dry up. He waits patiently for the most blessed moment of transcendent peace in the bosom of the eternal—beyond space, time and action. In the meantime he may engage in some deeds of virtue, regardless of consequences.

But a striking shift of emphasis in Indian thought was occasioned by the renaissance of Hinduism which started with Raja Ram Mohan Roy, Sri Ramkrishna, and Swami Dayananda. Affirmative and dynamic elements in the Hindu tradition were reaffirmed and strongly emphasized. In the ancient Vedic period of India the idea of bringing down the glory of the gods into human life and society was a major spiritual influence. In the Upaniṣads the reality of the world was affirmed as a diversified outflow of the fullness of joy in the heart of the Supreme Being (*Brahman*). In the Purāṇas the notion of the reign of truth in history (Satyayuga) was a source of inspiration; the ideal of living true to the kindred points of time and eternity was especially stressed. In the Bhagavadgītā the concept of the rule of law—the kingdom of truth and righteousness in human society (*dharmarājya*)—was the central theme of the whole teaching of Sri Kṛṣṇa.

The leading thinkers of modern India have reaffirmed such positive and dynamic conceptions of the spiritual ideal of life. In doing so they have laid the foundation for a harmonious blending of the highest cultural values of the traditional East and the modern West. They have indicated the lines along which India's spiritual know-how regarding man's union with the ground of existence may be fruitfully combined with the technical and political know-how of the West in improving the conditions of living in the world.

Sri Ramkrishna, the saint of Daksineswar, demonstrates the essential unity of all the great religions of the world. He declares that all religions, when followed with the sincerity of purpose and singleness of devotion, ultimately lead to the same goal of God-realization or integration with Being. But he also points out that the realization of the Supreme Being carries within it the imperative of selfless social service—the service of the Divine that dwells in the heart of man.

The great poet Rabindranath Tagore stresses the concept of creative freedom. He proclaims that freedom which is of the essence of the spirit in man is not freedom *from* society but freedom *in* society. It is in a thousand and one bonds of loving relationship with fellow beings that true freedom is to be enjoyed.

Mahatma Gandhi, the architect of India's national freedom, seizes upon two central concepts of Hindu ethics: truth and non-violence (*satya* and *ahiṁsā*). He believes that these are the common denominator of all historical religions. They represent the soul force which is vastly superior to the brute force of machine-guns and bombs and therefore capable of solving any political, racial or international problem. They are indispensable in transforming internecine power politics into the politics of human welfare and world peace.

The philosopher-statesman Sarvepalli Radhakrishnan stresses the concept of social salvation. The fate of individuals as well as of groups is inextricably linked up with the fate of the entire human family. So no individual can be completely liberated until the human race is liberated. No nation or people can reach its ultimate goal until humanity as a whole is ready for self-fulfilment. Different nations must therefore have an opportunity of growing freely within the framework of international harmony.

The silent sage Raman Maharshi emphasizes the need for critical self-inquiry and blissful self-poise. When the self begins to realize its essence, it may at the beginning have a feeling of withdrawal from the world of nature and society. It may at first experience the physical excluded from the trance-like awareness of the spiritual. But when self-awareness is sufficiently deepened, the gulf between the natural and the spiritual is overcome and one can blissfully abide in the Self in the midst of all the ordinary activities and pursuits of social existence. Spiritual self-integration becomes then a perfectly natural condition (*sahaja*).

The dynamic seer-philosopher Sri Aurobindo stresses the need for the integral experience of Being and a creative attitude to life. Integral experience of Being involves three factors: (1) union with the non-temporal dimension of existence (Śiva); (2) mobilizing the deepest powers and potentialities of the human psyche (*ātman*); and co-operation or creative fellowship with the evolutionary force of Being (Śakti). This concept of integral experience provides a broad basis upon which the insights of the aforesaid leaders of modern India may be unified in an all-embracing synthesis. Gandhi has demonstrated the value of truth and love as guiding principles in the work of the social and political reconstruction of life the world over. Aurobindo believes that this work of reconstruction can be enormously enhanced by mobilizing the hitherto-untapped and unsuspected resources of human personality and pressing them into the service of truth, love and creative evolution.

Integral Yoga is the art of harmonious and creative living on the basis of the integral experience of Being. It aims at opening the springs of creative inspiration hidden in the human psyche. It aims at that serenity of self-poise which preserves the light of the eternal amidst the storm and stress of social living. It aims at active participation in the being of the world with a view to the outflowering of the Divine in the march of civilization.

Integral experience is the basis of an integral world-view (*Weltanschauung*). Central to the integral viewpoint is the concept of multiform and multidimensional Being (*Brahman*). Being is the ultimate ground of all existence which different metaphysical systems and religious faiths try to express in different ways. The two inseparable aspects or dimensions of Being are: the transcendent eternal (Śiva) and the dynamic universal (Śakti). The dynamic universal is the creative energy of Being. It is productive of ever new forms, qualities, values, patterns of existence, levels of consciousness, etc. The world-process consisting of nature and history, matter and spirit, is the creative energy of Being in manifestation. The human self is an active centre of self-expression of Being, like a spark of fire issuing forth from the cosmic flame. It is capable of partaking on the one hand of the life eternal of Being, and participating on the other in the creative adventure of Being. Every human individual is essentially a child of immortality, a focalized expression of the vital urge. His purpose in life is to realize his authentic self as a unique centre of creative freedom, as an active source of new values, as a channel of expression of the hidden possibilities of Being. Integral Yoga is the art of such dynamic self-realization.

The present volume purports to present the essentials of Integral Yoga in a brief outline. It is not intended to be a summary of ideas embodied in any previous work or thought system. The author alone is responsible for the thoughts and interpretations set forth in the following pages. The essentials of integrated living have been developed by him in his own independent way. Metaphysical technicalities have been avoided as far as possible. English equivalents of Sanskrit terms have been mostly preferred with a view to making matters a little easy for the Western reader. Those aspects of Hindu philosophy and Sri Aurobindo's metaphysics which are too abstruse and yet not so necessary from the practical standpoint, have been left out of account (e.g. supernatural planes of existence, subtle distinctions between higher mind, illumined mind, intuitive mind, overmind and supermind, etc.).

In the first two chapters the true meaning of yoga has been elucidated and the significance of integral yoga has been brought out. Chapters III and IV make a brief critical survey of the traditional yoga systems of India. It is indicated how integral yoga represents a higher creative synthesis of the traditional ideals. In the original teaching of the Vedas and the Upaniṣads there was an optimistic affirmation of the world as an outflow of the fullness of joy in the heart of existence. In the monastic orders that grew out of the teaching of the Buddha and Śaṅkara there was a pessimistic emphasis upon world and life negation as a means to the highest spiritual fulfilment. Integral yoga harmonizes in a balanced synthesis the optimistic and pessimistic tendencies, the affirmative and negative attitudes to life. It renounces, not life and world, but man's blind attachment to them. It affirms, not the forces of greed and violence operative in life, but the deeper potentialities of life as a vehicle of truth and beauty and love. On the basis of such affirmation the evolutionary perspective of the modern West can be integrated into the framework of India's spiritual heritage.

Chapter V sketches the main principles of integral yoga, which is dominated by the ideal of man's integral union with the authentic self, the evolutionary world-spirit and the Supreme Being. Chapter VI embodies a brief outline of the philosophical basis of integral yoga. It affirms reality to be multi-form and multi-dimensional. The eternal, the dynamic universal and the unique individual are shown to be equally real aspects of the universe. The last two chapters are intended to meet the long-felt need for a comprehensive but succinct account of the most important methods of meditation as practised in India. It has been indicated how different techniques of spiritual practice can contribute to self-integration and creative freedom.

The author owes a debt of gratitude to the Mother, Sri Aurobindo Ashram, Pondicherry, for all her gracious help in grasping the essentials of Integral Yoga. Her kind permission to use in this book some quotations from the basic writings of Sri Aurobindo is thankfully acknowledged. Grateful thanks are also due to Dr Pitirim A. Sorokin, Director, Harvard Research Center in Creative Altruism, for kindly writing a Foreword for this volume.

The Author

San Francisco,
March 1964

CHAPTER I

THE MEANING OF YOGA

YOGA is a pivotal concept in India culture. It has been at the source of all significant religious and philosophical movements.

Philosophic thinking in India has been concerned from the very beginning with the root crisis of the spirit in man. The basic issue of human suffering including moral, religious and psychological problems has been traced to one ultimate cause, to wit, self-estrangement, alienation from existence, loss of contact with Being. Emotional conflicts, social discords, political wars—all these, in final analysis, flow from man's loss of contact with the ground of existence (*ātman* or *Brahman*). Alienation from existence makes him outwardly oriented to the point of restlessness. He eagerly looks for his happiness in the outside world. He fiercely fights for the blessings of life with rival contestants. He desperately searches for truth as an object of contemplation, as a thing to think about. He seriously endeavours to settle his accounts with fellow beings by means of objectivized principles, pacts and agreements. He forgets that the crux of his crisis lies within himself, in the buried discrepancies of his own nature. Yoga calls attention to this crucial fact. It aims at that vital existential experience which reunites man with the inmost centre of his own being.

No philosopher in India is accounted authentic unless he is also a yogi. A yogi is one who does not merely talk philosophy but lives philosophy. He does not simply have faith in God but experiences God. For him true philosophy is no mere intellectual pastime. Nor is it just otiose contemplation of the real. It must grow out of his existential experience and help him to intensify and broaden the base of such experience. For a yogi religion is not a mere system of faith or creed. It is a matter of personal realization or integration with reality. It is a matter of immediate contact with Being. Different religions are different pathways leading to this ultimate goal of existential contact.

In our present age the problem of man's alienation from existence has reached fearful proportions. Modern man is in great danger of being crushed by the machines he has himself created. He is in danger of being lost in the crowd. He is faced with the danger of being swallowed by authoritative institutions, giant corporations, and monstrous dictatorships. Intensified struggle for existence leaves him little time for coming to terms with his own inner self. Ideological conflicts and international tensions have vastly accentuated his sense of insecurity. Enlightened modern man can hardly fall back upon the mercy of the old gods, i.e. the traditional values of medieval thinking embedded in supernaturalistic dogmas and creeds. The old gods have died, even though the tragic news has not yet reached the orthodox and conservative segments of humanity. Not all those who have heard the news are quite aware of its full significance. The reassuring voice of the new gods is not yet clearly audible.

Yoga points to the truth beyond the gods of different races, nations and parochial religions. It affirms the reality of the Self (*ātman, puruṣa*) as the one beacon light in the enveloping darkness of conflicting creeds and ideologies. Yoga is existential appropriation of the truth. At its best it is also an act of manifold self-expression of the truth. We call that integral yoga, which we shall discuss at some length in the following chapters. On the basis of balanced union with the ultimate ground of existence, integral yoga aims at the reconstruction of life and society into a growing image of the truth. It stresses the need for creative action in harmony with the cosmic purpose of existence.

Unfortunately a huge amount of misunderstanding has grown around the notion of yoga. A good deal of malpractice has lent support to such misunderstanding. In the minds of many people yoga is associated with fortune-telling, crystal-gazing, glass-swallowing, fire-walking, etc. Some people associate it with such supernormal powers as levitation, clairvoyance, clairaudience, telepathy, thought-reading, etc. Let me relate here a little incident from my own personal experience. It was at San Francisco in May, 1951. I was waiting for a public bus at a street corner. An elderly man watched me from a distance and approached with the friendly inquiry: 'Are you from India?' On my replying in the affirmative, he promptly asked again: 'Are you a yogi?' I paused to think for a while what might be his notion of a yogi and why he took me for one. I was wondering what I should say to satisfy his inquisitiveness. But he did not wait for my reply. Perhaps he thought that since I was from India I must be a yogi. So he produced his palm before me and said, 'Would you care to read my palm and tell me whether I have any good luck in the near future? The other day I bought a good lottery ticket, you know.' That revealed to me at once what his idea of a yogi was. Many people in the West seem to share that idea. For this they are not altogether to blame. There have been many instances of impostors who have wandered around in the guise of yogis and have exploited the credulity and wishful thinking of common people.

Those who are a little better informed think of yoga as a system of bizarre physical postures and breathing exercises supposed to be helpful in attaining health, youth and longevity. Some think of it as the means of acquiring various occult powers of extrasensory perception. Some practise it as an aid to salvation or God-realization. What is frequently overlooked is that physical postures and breathing exercises do not belong to the essence of yoga. There are systems of yoga, e.g. those of contemplation (*jñāna*) and devotion (*bhakti*), which do not include these at all. They occupy a place in *haṭhayoga* and to some extent in *rājayoga*, but even in these systems they are intended only for some bodily preparation entitling one to take up higher phases of yogic practice such as concentration, meditation, and the like.

THE ESSENCE OF YOGA

What then is the essence of yoga? The word yoga is derived from the Sanskrit root-verb *yuj* meaning bind, join, unite, control. It is allied to the English word *yoke*, the German *joch*, and the Latin *jungo* (I join). Yoga thus literally means union and control. It signifies the union of man with God, of the individual with the universal reality, of each with the All of existence. It means union of the mortal with the eternal. It implies union of the mind with the inmost centre of one's own being, the self or *ātman*—union of the conscious mind with the deeper levels of the unconscious—resulting in the integration of personality. That is indeed the chief objective of yoga. But yoga also means control, that is to say, appropriate self-discipline. It is the mobilization of the inner resources of personality with a view to attaining that self-integration which religion calls God-realization, and mysticism calls immediate union with the infinite. In this sense yoga is the method or technique, the programme of psycho-physical, moral and spiritual training, by following which one can fulfil the ultimate destiny of life. The word yoga thus implies both the goal of life and the path leading to that goal. A yogi is one who follows the spiritual path of self-discipline, or who has attained the goal of self-realization.

A basic idea in yoga is that of freedom in spiritual self-expression. Yoga does not believe in any standardized path, for all to follow. It does not stand for any rigidly fixed rule, to which all should conform. It does not offer any patent remedy for human salvation. It affirms the oneness of truth, but rejects the uniformity of living. The fundamental conviction in yoga is that there are different psychological types to which people belong. There are introverts and extroverts; there are contemplatives and activists; there are the self-analytical and impulsive, emotional and intuitive types of people. It is therefore in the fitness of things that corresponding to these different psychological types there should be different lines of self-development, or different avenues of approach to creative self-expression. The important thing is that every individual should have the opportunity of growing from the roots of his own being, following the bent of his own nature, along the lines indicated by his own psychical make-up, towards the full flowering of his individuality as a unique creative centre of the cosmic whole.

YOGA AND RELIGION

The question is often asked, Is yoga a form of religion? What is the precise relationship between them?

It is a grievous mistake to think of yoga as a special form of religion as distinguished from other religions of the world. Every religion in its essence is regarded by a Hindu as a kind of yoga in so far as it helps man in attaining union with God or integration with existence. Yoga calls upon man to rise above all pet theories and dogmas and to set aside sectarian creeds and ritualistic observances. They erect barriers between man and man and create division and dissension in the name of love and unity. Yoga calls attention to the spiritual oneness of all mankind. Persons belonging to different religious faiths may profitably practise yoga without abandoning their particular religious affiliations and without having to undergo any new kind of religious baptism or credal conversion. For the practice of yoga it is not even necessary that a person must have faith in God, let alone any determinate conception of God. Even a sceptic or atheist may with profit practise yoga, provided only that he has a sincere desire to know the truth and a readiness to live up to his vision of the truth. The basic requirement of yoga practice is the sincerity of purpose and a resolute will to carry on open-minded investigation in the realm of the spirit.

If a person starts with some kind of religious faith, yoga aims at turning that faith into personal realization of the truth. Yoga is not a matter of belief; it is that inner growth of consciousness which results in direct insight into the heart of reality. It is not conformity to scriptural injunctions or some fixed socio-cultural pattern, but progressive realization of the full freedom of the inner spirit. It endeavours to turn doubt into critical self-inquiry and faith into living experience.

In a sense yoga is a kind of universal religion. That does not mean a universal system of dogmas and creeds. By the very nature of the case there can be no universal creed. All creeds are relative to different individuals and different communities. They are relative to the special circumstances of different geographical areas and historical epochs. Yoga is emphatic in its affirmation of the relativity of all creeds. They are relatively valid in helping different individuals and communities in attaining self-fulfilment on a reality basis. Yoga is universal religion in so far as it stresses the oneness of this ultimate goal of all spiritual effort. It lies in satisfactory integration with reality. It may also be described as existential assimilation of the truth.

One may also define yoga as a kind of universal spirituality beyond all religions. It is a non-religious spiritual orientation. It believes that when a Hindu achieves the ultimate objective of his spiritual effort, namely, integration with truth, he ceases to be a mere Hindu. Born as a Hindu he becomes a world citizen or cosmic man. When he reaches the goal of Hinduism he sees that this is also the ultimate goal of other great religions. Hinduism is thus fulfilled in his life beyond itself. Similarly, when a Christian reaches the ultimate goal of his sincere spiritual effort, he ceases to be a mere Christian. Human labels cannot restrict him any more. He becomes a cosmic man. The same is true of a sincere Buddhist, a sincere Muslim, etc. Different religions are like so many boats helping different peoples to cross the river of ignorance and self-alienation. When the other shore is reached, the boats are left behind. The content of wisdom for which the other shore stands is found to be identical. It is this concept of the identical spiritual destiny of man—this ideal of cosmic integration with the ground of existence—which is the basis of yoga.

YOGA AND ETHICS

How does yoga differ from ethics? Does yoga disregard the fundamental ethical distinctions of right and wrong, good and evil?

Ethical discipline is believed to be the first indispensable phase of yoga practice. It lays the foundation for higher self-development and deeper self-awareness. Patanjali, the celebrated ancient teacher of yoga, lays stress upon morality as an essential pre-requisite to the psycho-physical and spiritual training involved in yoga practice. Abstention from evil-doing (*yama*) and observance of noble principles (*niyama*) are the first two essential steps of his eightfold yogic path.[1] According to his teaching, one should not take up exercises in breathing, concentration, and the like, without first developing and strengthening the ethical consciousness through the practice of

[1] *The Yoga Sutras of Patanjali*, II, 30 and 32.

truthfulness (*satya*), non-violence (*ahiṁsā*), non-stealing (*asteya*), non-self-indulgence (*brahmacarya*) and non-greed (*aparigraha*).

But yoga is not the same thing as ethics. Just as it is universal spirituality beyond all credal religions, so it is self-luminous spirituality beyond all external ethical standards. Yoga looks upon ethics as an essential means to the fulfilment of a higher end, to wit, self-realization or integration with the ground of existence. Such self-realization is regarded as a supra-moral mode of existence. From the standpoint of yoga morality may be said to fulfil itself beyond itself, just as religion fulfils itself beyond itself. Morality is like a boat which helps in crossing the river—the river of ignorance and egoism—and reaching the other shore. The other shore is integration with the ultimate ground of existence. It puts an end to the sufferings of self-estrangement. It is the existential appropriation of truth, love, peace and freedom.

The boat is an essential means of transportation, but having reached the other shore nobody holds on to it in recognition of its usefulness. The right thing to do is to jump off to the shore and enjoy the freedom and fulfilment of landing there. In the scheme of self-development called yoga, morality is the foundation and an essential aid to growth. But the crowning achievement is spiritual freedom and spontaneous living which has been described as 'beyond good and evil' (*dvandvātīta*). Western scholars have frequently misunderstood this idea of 'beyond good and evil' in Hindu philosphy. So it would not be out of place here to discuss briefly the implications of the concept of supra-ethical self-realization or of virtue beyond good and evil.

First of all, a spiritually liberated person is supra-ethical not in the sense that he can indulge in immoral actions and injure the interests of society with impunity. By reason of his self-integration he becomes supra-ethical in the sense he is now by his nature incapable of doing anything harmful to human welfare. He serves society or humanity without any self-righteous feeling or any trace of egocentricity. Even his left hand does not know what his right hand is doing by way of helping others. He performs virtuous actions not out of any inner compulsion, nor out of any sense of moral obligation, nor out of a longing for meritorious action. He performs virtue unconsciously out of the free spontaneity of his integrated nature. He does good to others, not because he has to, but because he takes pleasure in doing so. The practice of virtue is with him the free outpouring of the self, the unmotivated self-giving of the inner spirit, like the shining of the sun or the blossoming of the flower.

Secondly, the supra-moral implies that man is not made for moral laws, but that moral laws are made for the constructive self-development of man in his individual and social nature. The precise meaning and application of such laws always depend upon the divergent socio-cultural contexts. People cannot be judged without reference to their background and motivation and the specific combination of circumstances in which they are placed at a given time.

A self-integrated person is supra-moral in the sense that his actions are not to be judged by ordinary standards of social morality. He has discovered a deeper principle of truth and love in his direct contact with Being. He may not often stand on ceremony in dealing with people. He may be unconventional in his mode of living. He may refuse to be impressed with the outward respectability of self-seeking people placed in high positions. He may act as a rebel. Society may condemn him or even crucify him on moral grounds. But still at the higher bar of truth and justice, he may be found vastly superior to those who crucify him.

When an ordinary person breaks a social custom or political law of the land, he is morally condemned on the ground that selfish motive obviously dictates his action. But when a man like Gandhi violates a social law (like dining with an outcaste) or a political law (like the imperialistic salt law), one has to suspend one's judgement until one knows better. All great spiritual masters like Socrates, Lao-tze, Buddha, Christ, Mohammed, Krishna, etc. have been in a greater or lesser measure supra-moral revolutionaries in their actions, much misunderstood by their contemporaries but hailed by posterity as architects of man's greater progress and welfare.

In the third place, a self-integrated person is beyond good and evil in the sense that he has transcended all conflicts and tensions within his own nature. So long as a man feels within himself a conflict between passion and reason, flesh and spirit, impulse and law, ego and super-ego, the ethical consciousness is acute and keen. But as soon as he succeeds in reducing his entire personality to a thoroughly organized and integrated whole, the conflict of good and evil is transcended in a unitary functioning of the total self. He lives and acts freely and spontaneously from the depth of his being. The idea of morality and virtue is in the foreground of consciousness only so long as the allurement or subtle suggestion of sin is there, lurking in the unconscious mind. As soon as this hidden allurement is eliminated through a thorough cleansing of the unconscious, virtue becomes second nature and ceases to be self-conscious. The opposition of impulse and law is transcended in the spontaneity of the spirit. Likewise, the opposition of ego and authority is transcended in the cosmic love of the true self (*ātman*).

Finally, the supra-ethical ideal of yoga implies that the ethical motive is subordinate to the dynamic spiritual perspective. In the initial stages of spiritual unfoldment the selfless service of society appears like a stern duty, an unconditional imperative. Love of the neighbour, love of humanity, is a divine commandment. But on the attainment of self-integration, one freely serves society as a matter of joyful self-expression. One then actively and spontaneously loves humanity as the diversified expression of the one cosmic self (*parama-ātman*) with which one is identified. Ethical action is then revealed no longer as an abstract duty nor as an unpleasant self-sacrifice. It is revealed as productive self-fulfilment in society. It is experienced as joyful self-expression and self-relating to the universe. The ethical motive is thus transformed into unfettered creative expression of the illumined consciousness. Through such transformation the ethical motive gains a new depth and a higher creative dynamism.

We are now in a position to observe that yoga is not ethics; it includes ethics and yet transcends it. Yoga does not believe in the absolute and unconditional validity of any ethical formulation. It does not believe in rigid conformity to any unalterably fixed ethical code. On the other hand yoga does not also deny the immense value and importance of ethical discipline for constructive self-development and social progress. For yoga, law is the body and freedom is the soul. Balanced self-discipline is the means, and self-integration is the goal. There is no freedom without law, but law may easily defeat its purpose by swallowing the spirit of freedom. There is no achievement without discipline, but discipline may easily become rigid and one-sided and thus defeat its purpose by mutilating personality. There is no growth without conformity to some regulating principle. But conformity to principle sometimes becomes a neurotic obsession, hindering further progress. In promoting spiritual growth, morality fulfils itself beyond itself. And it is the concept of free spiritual growth which is the main concern of yoga.

YOGA AND PHILOSOPHY

How is yoga related to philosophy? Is it based upon any particular philosophical system? Or, does it completely repudiate the value of all philosophizing?

Just as ethics is an essential factor in the practice of yoga, so also philosophy plays an important part in the scheme of self-development called yoga. Philosophy is an organized set of ideas regarding the meaning of life and the position of the individual in the total scheme of existence. There are different systems of philosophy, just as there are different systems of yoga, corresponding to different psychological types of people. Some kind of philosophical world-view (*Weltanschauung*) is essential for the release of the creative energies of the human soul. Yoga makes full use of this ideological apparatus for the constructive growth of personality, instead of pronouncing wholesale condemnation upon systematic philosophizing. But yoga does not believe that every individual must adopt the same kind of philosophical world-view. It is quite in the fitness of things that people belonging to different psychological types would need different kinds of philosophical formulation for their spiritual nourishment, intellectual growth and meaningful self-expression.

It is not a final and complete philosophy of life which is the goal of yogic practice. An unalterably fixed philosophical system is neither possible nor desirable nor necessary. It is not possible, because reality is essentially non-verbal and non-conceptual. The concrete fullness of reality can hardly be equated with any conceptual scheme of verbal symbols that philosophy is. In consideration of this fact attachment to an absolute philosophical system would be undesirable. It would produce dogmatism and detract attention from the need for existential experience. An absolute system is not also necessary in any way. What is vitally needed for human growth is relative truth, not absolute truth. The function of philosophy lies in providing useful intellectual tools for the growth of human personality eventually resulting in the immediate experience of reality. So in order to be useful and valuable for different psychological types it is only natural that there should be different relatively valid philosophical systems emphasizing and crystallizing such aspects of reality as would be stimulating, nourishing and inspiring to different individuals and groups.

Yoga then is not philosophy; it includes philosophy and yet transcends it. In the scheme of constructive self-development called yoga, a definite philosophical system appropriate to a particular individual plays a very significant and useful role. But as soon as the ultimate goal of yoga is attained, the individual goes beyond the furthest limits of that philosophical formulation which had been his sustaining creed for so long. Thus philosophy fulfils itself beyond itself. The seeker after truth now attains immediate contact with Being. The content of such immediate experience is, by its very nature, incapable of being adequately expressed within the four corners of a determinate philosophical system or rigid thought structure. Its expression in intellectual terms is bound to be conditioned by the prevailing intellectual climate and by the purpose and plan of action of the yogi in a given historical situation. But the inadequacy and relativity of philosophical world-views is no argument against their usefulness and validity.

Philosophical articulation of the immediacy of yogic experience is of paramount importance in various ways. It is an effective means of communication with fellow beings. It assists in sharing with them the treasures of spiritual insight. Secondly, philosophy is immensely helpful in comparing, correlating and arranging in a comprehensive picture the different levels of spiritual intuition and mystical experience. Thirdly, it can play a very constructive role in correlating and co-ordinating the facts of spiritual intuition with such other areas of human experience as aesthetic creation, moral action, scientific investigation, social organization, etc. Thus whereas yoga transcends philosophy in its advance towards supra-intellectual experience of pure existence, philosophy transcends yoga by bringing that experience into the sphere of rational communication and of the total organization of life and society.

In anticipation of our discussion in the following chapter a word may be added here about the concept of integral yoga. Traditional yoga looks upon ethics and philosophy as valuable aids to mystic realization and spiritual freedom. Therein lies its major emphasis. For integral yoga, ethics, philosophy and mysticism—action, knowledge and freedom—are inseparable moments in the total spiritual fulfilment of man.

We have seen that on the attainment of mystic union with existence ethics undergoes a radical change. The liberated person acts, no longer in conformity with any external standard, but freely out of the fullness of his love of man and God. He acts no longer out of any sense of obligation or inner compulsion, but on the basis of his luminous vision of the dynamic significance of society and civilization. Likewise, on the attainment of genuine spiritual freedom, philosophy loses its absolutism. No particular thought system such as materialism, idealism, realism, humanism, transcendentalism, etc. is equated any more with the absolute truth. The liberated man considers different philosophical systems as different perspectives of the same multi-dimensional reality. Each is important in its own way, but none can be said to utter the last word of wisdom. But this should be no justification for a life of floating indecision and inaction either. For an integral yogi philosophic contemplation loses its power as the siren song of distraction from the main business of living. In a given historical situation he chooses or develops a determinate thought system as the basis for action towards the fulfilment of his life mission in society. He has no dogmatic or finalistic illusion about his philosophical position. He perceives its value and usefulness in his service of man and pursuit of higher values. Thus an integral yogi is at once a mystic and a philosopher. He is at once a contemplative and an activist. Integral yoga reconciles the antagonistic principles of comprehensive thinking and existential choice—the principles of detached contemplation and loving participation in life.

YOGA AND PSYCHOLOGY

How is yoga related to psychology?

Psychology is a positive and empirical science of the mind in so far as the mind is knowable by methods of observation, experiment, and analysis. Yoga is the science of human personality in respect of its inner growth and creative self-fulfilment. It may be regarded both as a science and an art in so far as it includes in its approach both theoretical and practical motivations. As a science it is knowledge of the self in its totality. As an art it is the way of achieving the free growth and total fulfilment of the self. The self is understood in yoga as a multi-dimensional reality. It is not just the conscious rational mind, or the totality of conscious and unconscious mental phenomena, or the mind-body complex. It includes in its structure what Dr Pitirim A. Sorokin has called a 'supra-conscious component'.[1] This supra-conscious component of human personality is logically indefinable and certainly inaccessible to external observation and analysis. It is however capable of being immediately experienced and intimately known by methods of organized and harmonious living. Yoga stresses the need for such methods of living so that one can acquire thereby increasing insight into the nature and dynamics of the supra-conscious. The methodology of yoga includes not only the methods of introspection and detached self-observation, but also the techniques of dynamic self-transcendence, psycho-physical self-energizing, critical self-inquiry, altruistic love, selfless action, watchful relaxation, etc., which fall outside of the scope of psychology as an empirical study. These techniques will be briefly discussed in the last two chapters.

Yoga appears to be more metaphysical than psychological on account of its use of such concepts as the supra-conscious, the pure self (*puruṣa* or *ātman*), timeless experience (*samādhi*, *nirvāṇa*, etc.) and the like. Are not these concepts trans-empirical? Some fundamental yogic concepts are no doubt trans-empirical in so far as they go beyond external perception, sensuous observation, and ordinary introspection. But they are not trans-experiential. They are descriptive of the facts of self-awareness on deeper levels of personality. They stand for profound psychological experiences which are believed to be accessible to all qualified and trained seekers. It is therefore a grievous mistake to construe yogic concepts as imaginative hypotheses of metaphysical speculation or postulates of religious faith. They are empirical in the broader sense of the term. Because they are

[1] Dr Pitirim A. Sorokin (ed.), *Forms and Techniques of Altruistic and Spiritual Growth* (Boston: The Beacon Press, 1954), pp. v, vi.

verifiable in the context of direct personal experience by anybody who cares to verify them by following appropriate methods of investigation.

Yoga is the science of human personality in its integral unity. The human mind is not just a given fact or thing out there to be analysed into factual propositions. Nor is it on the other hand a mere idea or disembodied spirit fashioning utopean ideals and delivering unconditional imperatives. Neither naturalism nor rationalistic ethics can furnish us with the key to the structure of human personality. The human mind is a dynamic growth with its hidden aspirations and unsuspected potentialities—with its creative freedom and unseen sources of inspiration. So according to yoga true knowledge of the human spirit cannot be obtained by mere application of the so-called scientific methods. Such knowledge can be gained only in the course of integrated living and the inner growth of consciousness. It is inseparable from an existing individual's total response to life. Knowing here is inseparable from being, and being is inseparable from becoming.

Dr Indra Sen has rightly observed, 'Indian psychology is . . . not a natural science concerned with the "is" of mental life. It is also not a normative science concerned with the "ought", the ideal alone. It is, we might say, a science of the "becoming" of conscious life, that of growth from the actual "to the possible" '.[1]

Whereas modern western psychology is an empirical study of the psyche in its conscious and unconscious aspects, yoga is active participation in the creative growth and self-fulfilment of the psyche. Wisdom which grows out of such participation throws a new light upon many psychological problems. The self-exploration of yoga goes far beyond empirical psychology by disclosing such depths and heights of the psyche as are inaccessible to the methods of introspection, external observation and objective psycho-analysis. Yoga is the art of self-knowing through concentrated living and that of abundant living through increasing self-awareness.

YOGA AND MYSTICISM

Mysticism is one of the most slippery words in the English language. At its worst it means mystery-mongering, occultism, obscurantism, and the like. At its best it means immediate union with the ultimate ground of existence. We may consider here mysticism in its higher form and compare it with yoga.

[1] *Vide* Dr Indra Sen's article 'The Indian Approach to Psychology' in *The Integral Philosophy of Sri Aurobindo*, Chaudhuri & Spiegelberg (eds.), (London: George Allen & Unwin Ltd., 1960), p. 187.

Mystics in the best sense of the term are those who attain direct personal realization of the fundamental truth of existence, whether that truth be called God, Self, Void, Nothingness, Being, Silence, or the supreme Mystery. But mysticism does not involve any definite methodically chalked-out path by following which mystic realization may be achieved. Mystics often stumble into their strange and unusual experiences. Mysticism does not provide any technique for systematic organization of such unusual experiences or for their proper co-ordination with the ordinary non-mystic areas of human consciousness, sensuous, intellectual, moral, aesthetic and emotional.

Yoga implies faith in definite and systematic procedures by following which mystic experience of pure existence can be achieved. It shows a scientific spirit of investigation in the domain of the spirit or in the realm of the unconscious. It also believes in the need for a rational understanding of the interrelations that exist between mystic realization and other provinces of human experience.

Oftener than not mysticism sets itself in opposition to logic and philosophy. Intellect is condemned as a hindrance to mystical intuition. But yoga stands for that total self-integration in which the intellectual aspect of personality has to be satisfied no less than the emotional and volitional aspects. So it looks upon logic and philosophy as valuable aids to self-fulfilment. They are conducive to the clarification of ideas and the broadening of outlook. Yogic realization is not the negation but consummation of the intellectual quest for the existential truth. Intellect is fulfilled beyond itself in the ontological insight of the yogi.

Yoga in its integral form maintains that when mystical insight is carried sufficiently deep it becomes a great creative factor in human living. According to integral yoga the harmony of wisdom, love and action is the substance of complete mystic realization. It is 'skill in works'[1] in the sense that it is the art of acting on the basis of a dynamic self-poise in Being (*brāhmī sthiti*). Through union with Being, the integral yogi is united with the All of existence, with the world process. So he acts in the world in the spirit of cosmic love and comprehensive vision of truth. He participates in life on the basis of a balanced ontological outlook.

Traditional yoga has distinguished the mysticism of knowledge, love, meditation, action, etc. The ultimate goal of all of them is mystic union with Being. But such mystic union may be static or dynamic, partial or complete. When it fastens exclusively upon the timeless aspect of Being, it amounts to static realization. It encourages preoccupation with the eternal, somewhat to the neglect of the cosmic

[1] Sri Aurobindo, *Essays on the Gita* (New York: E. P. Dutton & Co., 1953), p. 93.

significance of time. But complete mystic union, which is the aim of integral yoga, involves an awareness of the cosmic meaning of time as well as a grasp of the eternal. It involves an understanding of the total structure of Being which includes the power of cosmic creativity (God) as well as the freedom of pure transcendence (Nothingness). Mystic awareness of transcendence and eternity bestows ineffable peace and freedom. Mystic awareness of the creative significance of time inspires active participation in life. The integral yogi participates in the evolutionary advance of time on the basis of a transcendent self-poise in the eternal. The integral yogi thus brings mysticism down to earth. He hears the voice of heaven in the evolving earth-consciousness of man. He feels the heart-beat of man in his striving for the kingdom of heaven on earth.

But is not this whole idea of man's mystic union with the Infinite philosophically untenable? Is not there an unbridgeable gulf between the finite and the infinite, between existence and transcendence?

The aforesaid problem is posed by the dualistic thinking of discursive reason. Yoga as higher mysticism is based upon a nondualistic outlook. Such dualisms as finite and infinite, existence and transcendence, are, in ultimate analysis, distinctions developed within the comprehensive unity of Being. They are relatively valid in so far as they designate different interrelated aspects of Being. But they do not represent irreconcilably separate segments of reality. Nor are they any argument against the interpenetrative continuum of the real.

From the nondualistic standpoint of Indian thought the infinite is not the opposite of the finite but its inmost centre and basis. The finite is a mode of manifestation of the infinite. So the finite can grasp the infinite by being one with itself. It does not, to be sure, know the infinite as an *object*, because the object falls outside of the subject. It knows the infinite by being aware of that ground of existence in which subject and object are united. Mystic union is not an external relationship. It is that non-relational experience in which both subject and object are transcended and unified.

Man can directly contact pure Transcendence because the transcendent is also immanent in him as the unifying centre of his existence. He contacts Transcendence through deeper self-awareness. The Transcendent is no doubt beyond nature and man, matter and spirit. But at the same time it is that ultimate unity in which they are unified. Nature and man are modes of manifestation of the same creative power of Transcendence. So the Transcendent is dynamically present in Nature as the universal life force. It also dwells in the heart of man as his inmost self.

Does man's mystic union with Transcendence amount to the

liquidation of his individuality? Is the mystic swallowed up in the fathomless depth of Being? Many western and Christian thinkers are terribly afraid of this prospect of self-loss in mystic union. The dualistic logic of either-or—either the individual or the transcendent—has lent support to this fear. The influence of this dualistic logic inherited from Aristotle has been so dominant in the western mind that it has not always fully grasped the significance of the teaching of Christ that it is by losing oneself that one can gain life everlasting. Resurrection of the spirit follows upon the crucifixion of the ego. Resurrection of the eternal and universal follows upon the crucifixion of the temporal-particular. When a man loses himself completely in Being, he is reborn in the depth of Being with all the glory of a divine child. What is annihilated is his egocentric individuality. But out of the ruins of the ego is born his true self. He is reborn as a cosmic man. He vividly realizes the oneness of all existence. He is also reborn as a uniquely creative personality. United with the centre of being, he glimpses the deeper significance of becoming. He joins forces with the creative flow of becoming. He becomes aware of the power of individuality as a source of new values and as a significant determinant of the world process. He freely co-operates with the cosmic creativity of Being.

Let us now turn to a brief discussion of the concept of the immediate in yogic mysticism. The idea of *immediate* union with Being has been misunderstood in various ways by western scholars.

Some think that the immediate experience of yoga is a regression to the primitive man's affective union with Nature. They call it the 'oceanic feeling'. It is the immediate feeling of kinship with the natural world of rivers and mountains, trees and animals. It is the original mode of existence of Adam and Eve in the garden of Eden. It is 'the undifferentiated aesthetic continuum' of sensuous immediacy.[1] It is the child's presentation-continuum—the 'big booming buzzing confusion'.

But the above is a complete misunderstanding of that supersensuous identity-consciousness (*samādhi*, *nirvāṇa*, etc.) which is the goal of yoga discipline. Yoga discovers a principle of unity beyond both sensuous immediacy and rational mediation. The primitive man's union with Nature was sensuous, affective or emotional union. He was submerged in the undifferentiated aesthetic continuum of the natural. So he had to break his emotional ties with Nature in order to discover himself as a spiritual entity—as man. The loss of paradise by Adam and Eve was therefore a big step forward towards spiritual self-development. Growth of the intellectual power of self-

[1] F. S. C. Northrop, *The Meeting of East and West* (New York: The Macmillan Company, 1950), p. 368.

consciousness and the ethical distinction of good and evil brought about this loss of contact with Nature. This was indispensable for the realization of the distinctive powers of man as man and for his mastery over Nature. In the course of further spiritual development man had similarly to break other emotional ties. For instance, he had to break the bonds of attachment to the father image and the mother image in his search for the self. He had to break loose from the fetters of tradition and authority in his undaunted spiritual adventure.

It is erroneous to think that yoga recommends the act of retracing these steps of civilization and going back to the original condition of the primitive man's sensuous and affective union with Nature. On the contrary, yoga stresses the need for gradual transcendence of all emotional ties—ties to home and soil and kith and kin—with a view to fully realizing the self. That is why the notions of non-attachment (*anāsakti*) and renunciation (*sannyāsa*) play a dominant role in the practice of yoga. But yoga believes that when a person discovers his inmost self (*ātman*), a deeper principle of unity in the heart of existence is disclosed to him. It is that transcendent unity of Being (*Brahman* or *Puruṣa*) of which sensuous immediacy and rational mediation are different modes of manifestation in the process of evolution. The undifferentiated aesthetic continuum and the differentiated structure of logical thinking are different phases of the creative self-expression of Being. Yogic immediacy is not a retrograde movement to the pre-logical and pre-ethical mode of infantile sensuous-emotional experience. On the contrary it is an advance through self-integration to a kind of supra-logical insight into the comprehensive unity of Being. It involves an act of self-transcendence beyond subject-object polarization. It aims at that supra-relational immediacy of which modern western philosophers like F. H. Bradley and Bernard Bosanquet had some inkling.

Some have argued that mystic union with Being is nothing but wish-fulfilment of the undying child in man. The growing individual always retains an unconscious nostalgic longing for the paradise of childhood union with the father or mother. There may even be a hidden longing for re-entry into the absolute peace and protection of the mother's womb. Is mysticism a sort of sublimated fulfilment of that longing? If so, is it not void of any ontological significance?

Let us assume for argument's sake that mysticism is sublimated fulfilment of an unconscious longing for the lost paradise of childhood. But does that necessarily knock out the ontological significance of the resulting experience of reunion with existence? The most remarkable thing about life is that one thing here always leads to another. A miraculous process of transformation is continuously going on in the creativity of Nature. Coal turns into diamond, mud turns into rose, soil into rich crops. Hydrogen and oxygen mixed in definite proportions produce water. But it is sheer stupidity to suggest that water is *nothing but* hydrogen and oxygen. What emerges out of them is an entirely new category, an emergent value. Carbon, hydrogen, oxygen and nitrogen combined in a specific configuration give rise to the living protoplasm. But it is sheer stupidity to suggest that life is *nothing but* physical and chemical forces. The living protoplasm is in truth a qualitative novelty, a unique emergent value. It represents a new dimension of reality radically different from physical and chemical forces.

A man who has been bitterly disappointed in his love affairs turns heart and soul to the mistress of art or science. He obtains sublimated fulfilment of the frustrated erotic impulse in his exalted experience of truth or beauty. It is sheer ignorance to suggest that truth and beauty as revealed to the scientist and the artist are devoid of any ontological significance. They are in fact higher emergent values in human experience. They represent entirely new dimensions of reality.

Similarly a man's nostalgic longing for the lost paradise may kindle a new fire in his soul. It may stimulate and awaken deeper powers of his consciousness. It may inspire in him a sustained effort to be reintegrated with existence on a higher plane of consciousness. He carries on this effort through a re-organization of his whole being in accordance with a central purpose. The resulting experience of mystic union with Being represents a new emergent value. It affords a deep insight into the timeless dimension of existence. At the touch of the eternal the human individual blossoms to the full just as a flower breaks into bloom at the touch of sunlight.

When Christ says: 'I and my Father in heaven are one,' he voices a profound yogic experience. In this experience the child in the human unconscious certainly obtains a new fulfilment. But it is fulfilled on a higher level of personality development. It is fulfilled through the discovery of a deeper principle of unity in life and a higher creative power. When a Vedāntin says 'I am essentially one with Being (*Brahman*)' he gives voice to his experience of existential contact with the eternal. He experiences the rootedness of his existence in the comprehensive unity of Being. His experience is neither sensuous nor intellectual nor emotional. It is the total experience of his total self in response to the total universe. It is the ontological awareness of his integrated personality.

Likewise when a Rājayogi says: 'I am one with the inmost centre of my being (*puruṣa*),' he expresses his discovery of the ultimate unifying principle of life—the self or the spirit in man. In making this discovery the individual is reborn on a higher plane of existence.

Not only the child in him—his nostalgic longing for reunion with Being—is satisfied here. He now experiences reality in its deeper unity by the power of his integrated personality. He is reborn as a new child, as a divine child, as an offspring of the integration of such divergent aspects of his nature as the intellectual and the emotional, the discursive and the intuitive. He recaptures the freshness and spontaneity of childhood through a contact with the deathless fire of life.

CHAPTER II

THE AIM OF INTEGRAL YOGA

ŚRĪ KṚṢṆA says in the Bhagavadgītā that a true yogi is a person who is dynamically united with the Divine in the field of action. The yogi is superior to the ascetic, the contemplative and the ritualist.[1] Yoga is essentially an act of dedication to the cosmic purpose of existence, the spiritual destiny of life.

It is this dynamic conception of yoga which has been carried to its full logical development in integral yoga (*pūrṇa yoga*). When a man's union or existential contact with Being becomes integral (i.e. balanced and complete), he is transformed into a dynamic personality. Integral vision of the truth turns him into a creator of new values. It inspires him to participate in life with a new sense of urgency and a new grasp of meaning.

The distinctive goal of integral yoga will be briefly outlined in this chapter in the background of the traditional yoga systems of India.

Integral yoga may be defined as the art of harmonious and creative living. It stresses the need for the balanced growth of personality; for constructive development of the latent possibilities of one's nature; and for their employment in the service of mankind and such higher values as truth, justice, freedom, peace and progress. Integral yoga warns against extreme tendencies which mislead people into lopsided development.

There are some who develop muscles at the cost of brains. There are some who over-exercise their brains much to the neglect of the body. Some again practise deliberate self-mortification and disparage both the physical and the intellectual in their search for the soul. There are some who are so much bent upon self-development that they ignore the social and humanistic values of life. On the other hand there are some who are so much entangled in social activities that suppressed emotional conflicts undermine their personal peace as well as social efficiency. There are some who follow the voice of God by rejecting the world. On the other hand there are some who get enmeshed in the affairs of the world without any idea of the eternal in man. Integral yoga sets forth the concept of the full flowering of the total individual as a dynamic centre of the universal spirit—the

[1] *The Bhagavadgītā*, VI, 46.

power of Being. It emphasizes the need for a balanced integration of the physical, emotional, intellectual, ethical, and religious aspects of personality.

LIFE AND YOGA

The whole course of our life is a striving for the realization of higher values. Values represent the riches of Being, its dynamic potentialities. Life springs from the depths of Being and presses forward towards the fulfilment of the various possibilities of Being. Thus whether we are aware of it or not, the whole movement of life is in a sense a process of yoga. It flows in union with the creative purpose of Being. It evolves in the direction of deepening awareness of that purpose. The more a person advances in life the deeper is his insight into the cosmic purpose of Being and its hidden possibilities.

The practice of yoga in the strict sense of the term is a resolute will to allow the power of Being to work more and more freely within us. It is a commitment to higher spiritual values. Ordinary life is a slow and meandering movement unconsciously determined by the cosmic power. Yoga is intelligent co-operation with that power in full measure. It is an acceleration of the tempo of life's process occasioned by a sort of Copernican revolution in the field of consciousness, i.e. by a transition from the egocentric to the cosmo-centric outlook.

Now, there are different levels of cosmic awareness. There are different modes of apprehension of the cosmic whole. It has been rightly observed: 'Being is one although sages call it by different names.'[1] But the unity of Being is not a blank featurless unity. It is a manifold and multi-coloured unity. It has an infinite richness of content and an endless diversity of forms, aspects and modes of manifestation. Different truth-seekers have approached it from different directions, differently motivated, differently equipped. Some have beheld it as the personal God and some have perceived it as the impersonal Truth. Some have known it as the spirit of Nature, and some have glimpsed it as the reality of Supernature. Some have regarded it as the total Fact and some have envisaged it as the supreme Value. Some have defined it by the concept of Equality whereas some have conceived it in terms of the ideal of Freedom.

According to integral yoga all the aforesaid views represent different perspectives of the same Being. Each perspective brings to light a certain facet of Being. And each perspective has some value and importance for some people in certain circumstances. But no perspective can be said to exhaust the concrete fullness of Being. No thought system or scheme of values can possibly express the whole and final truth. It is like the same elephant appearing as a pillar to

[1] *Ṛg Veda*, X, 14.

some blind person; as a wall to some; as a serpent to some; as a fan to some. These limited tactual perceptions are unified in the total vision of the elephant. But no blind man has that total vision. Likewise no human ideology or value system can encompass the multiform fullness of Being.

The history of Indian culture is full of endless experiments with the truth in the sphere of living. All conceivable paths have been explored for unveiling the nature and purpose of Being. *Haṭhayoga, Rājayoga, Karmayoga, Jñānayoga, Bhaktiyoga—Vedāntism, Vaiṣṇavism, Tāntricism* including *Śaivism* and *Śaktism*, the *Hīnayāna* and *Mahāyāna* schools of Buddhism—are some of the most noteworthy of such spiritual experiments. Yoga is the general name for these experiments; it is the art of living in harmony with the fundamental truth of existence. Understood in this sense genuine mystics in other parts of the world can also be called yogis. Neo-Platonists, Taoists, Jewish and Christian mystics, Sufis, Zen Buddhists, etc. can be said to have followed the path of yoga with marvellous results. Following the principle of cosmic integration they have been able to gain deep insights into the heart of existence.

It is of vital importance today that the ontological insights embodied in the highest spiritual experiences of mankind should be given a practical and dynamic form. Dedicated souls the world over should discover a common meeting ground and a way of sincerely co-operating towards the fulfilment of the common destiny of man. They have to mobilize the spiritual resources of man in solving his most crucial problems, to wit, the problems of human unity, peace and progress. Integral yoga is concerned with such human co-operation and spiritual mobilization. It is an appeal to the religious impulse of man for active participation in the evolutionary advance of life on the basis of balanced self-integration.

INADEQUACY OF THE ASCETIC IDEAL

Like the religious approach of the West in the Middle Ages, the yoga systems of India during the medieval period were largely inspired by the ascetic ideal of transcendent liberation. They were largely life-renouncing and world-negating. All the evils and sufferings of life were traced to our subjection to the cosmic creative principle. Some defined this cosmic principle as unconscious Nature. Some defined it as the cosmic principle of ignorance or nescience. Some conceived it as the unconscious will or ignorant desire. But they were all agreed on one point, namely, that our existence is a condition of entanglement in the wheels of the cosmic drive. It is blind identification with the vital impetus. All suffering flows from this identification. The way to eternal bliss would therefore consist in an act of disentanglement from the cosmic drive. Renunciation of all social bonds is the one great exit from the deceptive merry-go-round of life.

The goal of spiritual effort has been conceived in Patanjali's yoga as transcendental loneliness (*kaivalya*).[1] It is the condition of self-abiding in separation from the world of action and reaction, claim and counterclaim, pain and pleasure, sustained by Nature (*Prakṛti*). The Vedāntin has conceived the ultimate goal as absorption in the eternal (Brahman-laya).[2] It is the awareness of the one eternal spirit as the only reality, the world of many individuals being an illusory superimposition thereupon. The Buddhist has conceived it as an indescribable spiritual condition beyond both existence and non-existence.[3] It is the awareness of the evanescence of life and the emptiness of the eternal.

Thus we see that the most dominant spiritual ideals of medieval India deprecated the value of life and the cosmic flow. They considered ignorance (*avidyā*) as the root cause of social, economical and political action. They overemphasized the notions of renunciation and ascetic negation. They glorified eternity by denouncing the march of time as the movement of ignorance. But that was in striking contrast with the affirmative and optimistic outlook of the Vedic, Upaniṣadic and Purānic sages of India. The Upaniṣads declared that the world came into existence out of the fullness of joy in the heart of Being.[4] Life in the world is therefore not a movement of ignorance but an adventure in the diversified expression of creative joy. The Purānas proclaimed that the highest goal of life was to act in this world, true to the kindred points of time and eternity. The timeless perspective which is the essence of spiritual wisdom makes a man free, curing him of egotism and aggressiveness. But it also lays the groundwork for perfect action. He is now in a position to participate in life as a perfect instrument of the values of eternity. This is the advice which the great Hindu sage Bṛhaspati gave to the lord Indra as related in *Brahmavaivarta Purāṇa*.[5]

Integral Yoga reaffirms the original Hindu ideal of participating in life as an instrument of the eternal. It holds that mere emancipa-

[1] Swami Sivananda, *Raja Yoga* (Rishikesh: The Yoga Vedanta Forest University, 1950), pp. 371–2.

[2] Swami Madhavananda, *Viveka-Chudamani of Sankaracharya* (Mayavati: Advaita Ashram, 1944), p. 160.

[3] H. D. Bhattacharya's article 'Early Buddhism' in *History of Philosophy, Eastern and Western*, S. Radhakrishnan *et al.* (eds.), (London: George Allen & Unwin Ltd., 1957), p. 166.

[4] Taittiriya Upanisad, III, 6.1.

[5] Heinrich Zimmer, *Myths and Symbols in Indian Art and Civilization* (New York: Pantheon Books, 1953), pp. 3–11.

tion from the bonds of the cosmic drive (*prakṛti* or *māyā*) is an incomplete spiritual ideal. Such emancipation has to be given a positive content. It is the beginning of a new life of action. It lays the foundation for enlightened participation in the creative joy of the world-spirit or the Divine in history. According to integral yoga, it is not enough to attain self-realization; there is a much nobler goal of human effort, and that is to achieve self-manifestation, that is, to apply in the sphere of daily living and social action the light and power of deeper self-awareness. It is not enough to gain liberation from unconscious Nature; there is a much sublimer goal of human endeavour, and that is to liberate Nature herself in the growing fulfilment of the creative urge concealed in her breast.

Those who are enamoured of the medieval ideal of liberation follow the path of negation. They follow the *via negativa* of the mystics or the *neti neti* (not this, not this) of the traditional yogis. They choose to rise higher and higher until the highest point is reached from which there is no coming back. Integral yoga stresses the need for supplementing ascent by descent, negation by deeper and fuller affirmation. One has surely first of all to climb the path of ascent and rise to the height of inward illumination. But if one is to participate in the creative joy of Being, one has to know how to correlate the upward movement of human aspiration with the downward movement of the timeless spirit. Having reached the height of his vision of the eternal, the integral yogi strives to express in the flux of time the glories of eternity. Having glimpsed the creative light of Being on a higher plane of consciousness, he descends into the physical and social spheres with a view to reconstructing human existence in accordance with that light. Ascent and descent are then two inseparable aspects of the movement of integral yoga; they are the systole and diastole of integral self-discipline. 'Our yoga,' says Sri Aurobindo, 'is a double movement of ascent and descent; one rises to higher and higher levels of consciousness, but at the same time one brings down their power not only into mind and life, but in the end even into the body. And the highest of these levels, the one at which it aims, is the Supermind. Only when that can be brought down is the divine transformation possible in the earth-consciousness.'[1]

TRANSFORMATION OF EXISTENCE

The followers of the exclusive path of ascent look upon body, life and mind as forming a sort of ladder which has to be used for climbing up to the summit of spiritual enlightenment. But after the summit is reached the ladder may be kicked aside. It is no use hold-

[1] Sri Aurobindo, *The Riddle of This World* (Pondicherry: Sri Aurobindo Ashram, 1951), pp. 2–3.

ing on to the ladder or climbing down it, except temporarily for showing other people the way to use it properly. But for integral yoga, body life and mind are not simply means of rising up to the highest peak, but also means of bringing down below and expressing here and now the glory of the spirit. They are not to be treated as a mere ladder but must be prepared as channels of expression of higher values in the world. In order that they may function effectively in that capacity, integral yoga insists that the dynamic truth-consciousness should be made operative in all of them. All the parts of our existence including even the physical and the darkest subconscious must be opened to the transmutive power of the light of Being. Herein lies the unique characteristic which distinguishes integral yoga from the traditional systems of religious discipline.

Traditional mystics, yogis and religious seekers looked upon the body as a burden upon the soul. Plato regarded the body as a prison-house for the free and immortal soul. Some mystics considered the body as an incorrigible abode of evil and sin, of passion and temptation. Ascetics looked upon the body as a necessary evil which must be discarded on the attainment of spiritual liberation. This pessimistic attitude of traditional spirituality encouraged the widespread practice of bodily torture, austerity and self-mortification as a means of spiritual advancement. It released the masochistic and escapist tendencies latent in human nature.

Integral yoga looks upon the body as an immensely valuable means of self-fulfilment and self-expression. The so-called passions and impulses of the flesh are the source of elemental energy. The vital impulses should not be suppressed or eliminated but intelligently organized and lawfully satisfied. Through such organization and satisfaction they have to be constructively channelled towards the realization of the higher ends of life. To torture or mutilate the body in the name of religious growth is an infantile procedure. The body has to be adequately developed and strengthened, not of course just for its own sake, but for the sake of the spirit. It has to be carefully built up as a powerful and effective means of serving the higher values of existence. Even after the full realization of the Divine, the body has to be used as an instrument for expressing the divine will in society. To that end it can be more and more purified, strengthened and transformed by the higher powers of consciousness.

DYNAMIC UNION WITH BEING

The second distinctive feature of integral yoga lies in the concept of dynamic union with Being. It is conscious and active integration with the ultimate ground of existence.

Traditional mysticism has always emphasized the notion of direct union with the eternal. Hinduism has called it *samādhi*. Buddhism has called it *nirvāṇa*. Christian mystics have called it 'unitive consciousness', 'cosmic consciousness', etc. This unitive consciousness has frequently been conceived as a kind of supra-physical exalted state of consciousness. The mystic loses here his contact with the outside world. And he finds here a revelation of the unreality of the material world or the natural order.

But integral yoga maintains that such an exalted matter-negating type of mystic vision is only a passing phase of the spiritual quest, and certainly not the goal. After the content of such transcendental realization is thoroughly assimilated, the barrier between the physical and the spiritual is removed. The mystic then acquires what may be called 'waking union with the Divine'. He brings down the wisdom and joy of transcedence right into the heart of his physical consciousness. He maintains the inner peace and blissful self-poise even while engaged in the ordinary activities of life such as eating, walking, talking with people, etc. The serenity of *samādhi* becomes his second nature. The barrier between the natural and the supernatural breaks down. Through integral union with Being the natural-material is revealed to him as a diversified expression of the creativity of Being.

Moreover, mystic union in integral form becomes dynamic. It changes the mystic into a creative personality. He cannot rest content with his own inner peace and joy any more. He participates in the creative adventure of life and evolution with a view to realizing higher values. Inwardly he is integrated with the ground of existence; outwardly he is engaged in all manner of activities for the good of humanity and in the best interests of human progress. He can maintain the perfect serenity of self-poise even while occupied with fighting with such forces of evil as despotism, tyranny, social injustice, racial prejudice, etc. Such dynamic union with the ground of existence is an essential factor in complete self-realization. It is the power of functioning wholeheartedly in life as an instrument of truth and justice. It is the free and spontaneous outflow of the inward realization of the cosmic purpose of existence.

COLLECTIVE LIBERATION OF MANKIND

The third essential characteristic of integral yoga lies in the concept of the collective liberation of mankind. Personal salvation is not the highest end. It is the means to a still higher end, namely, the liberation and transformation of human society—'the outflowering of the Divine in collective humanity'. Integral yoga aims at mobilizing the spiritual resources of human personality towards the establishment of one world-order characterized by peaceful co-existence, constructive co-operation, and an increasing realization of higher values.

Many people follow the spiritual path with a view to attaining personal salvation. Having attained liberation for themselves, they live in complete or partial solitude and retirement. The utmost they may do for the sake of others is to render some help to isolated individuals who come to them for spiritual comfort and guidance. They do not concern themselves with the social, historical or evolutionary life of humanity. This is the ideal of the solitary mystic, the lonely pilgrim of the infinite. In Buddhism this is known as the ideal of the *Pratyekabuddha*.[1] He endeavours to shine as a lamp unto himself.

A greater spiritual ideal affirms the goal to be the collective liberation of mankind. In Vedānta it has been called *sarva-mukti*.[2] No individual, however enlightened and inwardly perfected he may be, can attain final liberation from the bonds of the cosmic process until the whole of humanity is ready to attain such liberation. This is because different individuals are closely interrelated and interdependent. They inseparably belong to the same cosmic whole or human family. Until the supreme moment of collective redemption arrives, spiritually enlightened individuals continue to live and act for the good of humanity. After their physical death they continue to function on subtler and higher planes of consciousness, rendering help in various ways to the struggling and suffering members of the living creation. Or, it is believed, the liberated souls may also freely choose to be reborn on earth in order to serve society in the best interests of man's spiritual progress.

The concept of collective liberation in Buddhism is known as the *Bodhisattva* ideal. It is the corner-stone of Mahāynāna Buddhism. It draws inspiration from the supreme act of self-sacrifice on the part of the great master Buddha. The Buddha's first act of sacrifice was the renunciation of all personal comfort and emotional ties. As his heart cried out at the sight of human suffering he renounced his family and kingdom in search of the ultimate meaning of life. After a long period of critical inquiry and meditation he obtained supreme enlightenment. He gained perfect integration of personality, spiritual freedom, *nirvāṇa*. Negatively speaking, *nirvāṇa* implies 'the blowing out' of the fourfold fire of ignorance, desire, egoism and anguish.

[1] S. B. Das Gupta, *An Introduction to Tantric Buddhism* (Calcutta: University of Calcutta, 1950), p. 9.

[2] S. Radhakrishnan, *The Brahma Sutra* (London: George Allen & Unwin Ltd., 1959; New York: Harper & Brothers, 1960), p. 218.

Positively speaking, *nirvāṇa* is the harmony of wisdom, compassion and peace.

In course of time the Buddha was finally brought to the doorstep of the highest spiritual bliss, the bliss of absorption in pure Transcendence. In Buddhist terminology, that was *parinirvāṇa* or *nirviśeṣa nirvāṇa*, meaning undifferentiated unification with the ultimate. But at that moment the Buddha paused for a while and retraced his steps. He made the supreme sacrifice of man's deepest longing for reabsorption in the abyss of transcendence. He firmly resolved to dedicate himself to the service of humanity toward their final redemption. The Buddha said: 'By entering into *parinirvāṇa* I may gain eternal peace and supernal joy, but for all practical purposes I shall be lost to suffering humanity. So I am taking this vow today that I shall not stop working and serving until every suffering member of the living creation is liberated from ignorance and passion and admitted into the realm of light and love and peace.' This is the great *Bodhisattva* vow. The Enlightened One continued to work indefatiguably for the good of mankind.

In Christianity there is a corresponding ideal of man's collective liberation. It is the concept of the kingdom of heaven. Jesus Christ had the vision of the coming of the supernatural kingdom of truth and love and justice. He felt that the natural order of existence was full of evil, sin and consequent suffering. It was dominated by the undivine power of Satan. But Christ had living faith in the infinitely superior power of God, the heavenly Father, who would eventually subdue the evil influence of Satan. Those who accept him and follow his teaching would be able to gain entrance into the kingdom of heaven. Those who fail to accept him or are opposed to him would eventually perish or be excluded from the kingdom of heaven.

The supernatural kingdom of heaven has been conceived by some as a blissful mode of existence beyond the grave. People with active faith in Christ would be admitted into the heavenly order after physical death. But others have visualized the kingdom of God as the ultimate meaning of human history. The natural order is the abode of evil, temptation and suffering. It is ruled by sex, ego, mammon and lust for power. So it is destined to be destroyed. The supernatural kingdom of God was going to be established on earth on the ruins of the natural order. The kingdom of perfection 'will be brought about by a cosmic catastrophe through which evil is to be completely overcome'.[1]

A brief comparison of the Buddhist and Christian views of man's collective liberation may be instructive at this point. Both affirm

[1] Albert Schweitzer, *The Mystery of the Kingdom of God* (New York: The Macmillan Company, 1957), p. 58.

the superiority of the ideal of collective liberation over that of personal salvation. Consequently, both recommend the principle of self-sacrifice for the sake of cosmic welfare. Both Mahāyāna Buddhism and medieval Christianity have been pessimistic and other-worldly. They have looked upon the natural order of existence as the above of evil and suffering, fit to be rejected. The life of passion and power-drive leads to perdition. Material values such as money, social position, political power, procreation, etc. are to be renounced as a positive hindrance to spiritual growth. Therefore the monk ideal rose into pre-eminence. Life in the monastery came to be regarded as the highest form of spiritual existence.

Let us now note a few differences. In Christianity the kingdom of heaven has been conceived in theological terms as a supernatural order ruled by a personal heavenly Father. In Mahāyāna Buddhism collective *nirvāṇa* has been conceived in philosophical terms as a state of enlightened and blissful reintegration with the ultimate ground of existence (suchness or emptiness). In Christianity the distinction between believers and non-believers has been particularly stressed. Only those who have faith would be entitled to enter the kingdom of heaven. Obstinate non-believers would perish. In Buddhism as well as in Hinduism the perfectibility or spiritual potentiality of all human beings has been recognized. All men are essentially children of immortality. Buddha-nature is present in the all of existence. So in the course of evolution all individuals, regardless of their present ideas and beliefs, will eventually discover the path of peace and immortality.

In Christianity the kingdom of heaven has in the main been conceived either eschatologically as an exalted mode of existence beyond the grave, or historically as the replacement of the rule of Satan in this world by the reign of God. In Buddhism as well as in Hinduism collective liberation has been conceived either psychologically as a state of supreme enlightenment and cosmic perspective, or evolutionarily as the crowning fulfilment of the cosmic process. In the latter case the natural order is not destroyed but fulfilled on a higher level. With man, nature also is as it were liberated. Indian thought never posited any absolute antagonism between nature and spirit. In Greek thought the serpent has to be killed so that the Greek hero Hercules may establish his superiority.[1] Christ also achieved triumph by crushing the serpent's head. But in Indian thought the serpent symbolizing the spirit of nature is not killed but transformed. The serpent is turned from an enemy into a friend by the power of wisdom and non-violence. When the Buddha attains his supreme

[1] Heinrich Zimmer, *Myths and Symbols in Indian Art and Civilization* (New York: Pantheon Books, 1953), p. 89.

enlightenment, all the genii of nature including the serpent, the principal personification of the waters of terrestrial life, rejoice, together with the highest gods.[1] Similarly the Hindu god Śiva achieves his triumph by subduing and transforming, and not by destroying, the monstrous serpent which attacks him.[2]

COLLECTIVE LIBERATION AS THE REIGN OF RIGHTEOUSNESS ('DHARMA')

The concept of collective liberation acquires a new depth of meaning in the teaching of the *Bhagavadgītā*.

In Christianity the supernatural kingdom of heaven is radically different from the world, the natural order, which is sinful. It can therefore be established on earth only on the ruins of the natural order. In Buddhism the spirit of nature also is fulfilled on man's attainment of *nirvāṇa*. But both nature and man obtain liberation in a transcendent sphere. The cosmic process is valuable only in so far as it eventually leads to the transcendent. It has no intrinsic value and significance of its own. But the divine teacher in the *Gītā* declares that the cosmic process has an intrinsic significance. It is not intended only as an ante-chamber to the glorious realm of transcendence. It is a meaningful sphere of manifestation of Transcendence. There is no radical opposition between the cosmic process and Transcendence. Nor is there any radical opposition between nature and history. Both nature and history, which are different aspects of the cosmic process, are modes of manifestation of the same world-spirit, the creative power of Transcendence. Collective liberation means the establishment of the transcendent values of truth and justice (*dharma*) on earth and in society. It is the incarnation of the eternal in time. This is the content of the divine will operative in history.[3] The reign of righteousness would not mean the abolition or destruction of the natural values of wealth, health, sex, ambition, power, etc. They would just be transformed into spiritually illumined forces. Thus the *Gītā* sets forth the balanced spiritual ideal of participation in life in union with the creative power of Transcendence or Being. Let us call it the integral ideal.

The integral ideal can be traced in germinal form in the ancient writings of the *Vedas* and the *Purāṇas*. The seers of the *Vedas* made sacrifices (*yajña*) to Gods for the manifestation of the divine glory in their collective social existence. They prayed for the divine powers

[1] Ibid, p. 66.

[2] Ananda K. Coomaraswamy, *The Dance of Shiva* (New York: The Noonday Press, 1959), p. 69.

[3] *The Bhagavadgītā*, IV, 7 and 8.

to be operative in a spiritual transformation of society. 'It is a continual self-offering of the human to the divine and a continual descent of the divine into the human'[1] which was the motivating factor in Vedic sacrifice.

The outline of the integral ideal becomes still clearer in some Purānic writings. A beautiful Purānic story[2] illustrating this point may be recalled here. Once upon a time Indra, the lord of the upper region, became very ambitious. He was all the time enlarging his plans for the expansion and beautification of his kingdom. Ever new ideas were streaming into his mind. This naturally imposed mounting strains upon his executive officers. One day by the grace of God, Indra was suddenly disillusioned. He clearly saw through the vanity of ego-striving and foolishness of excessive ambition. He realized the evanescence of life and had a glimpse of the timeless dimension of existence. A profound change came upon him. From over-ambitious activism he was now swung to the opposite extreme of retiring asceticism. He began to think in terms of renouncing his kingdom and family and burying himself in quiet contemplation of the eternal. At that moment his spiritual counsellor Brihaspati intervened. He stressed the need for balance and integration. He set forth the ideal of being true to the kindred points of heaven and home, eternity and time. He taught that the balanced spiritual ideal has two inseparable aspects, inward and outward. Inwardly, an individual has to be integrated with the eternal and thus rise above personal greed and vanity, insatiable lust and acquisitiveness. But to reject life on gaining the timeless perspective is another form of ignorance. The process of time, of evolution, of history, is no less significant. It is the medium of manifestation of the free creativity of the eternal. So the supreme spiritual task lies in joyful participation in the creative flow of life and time. It consists in selfless performance of duties and responsibilities on the basis of one's dynamic vision of eternity.

This idea of enlightened participation in life in union with the eternal has been presented in a more dramatic manner in the *Gītā*. Arjuna, the human hero, is placed at the centre of the battlefield of Kurukṣetra. He is the leader of those who believe in the rule of law, in the supremacy of truth and justice. The opposing camp consists of those who are bent upon establishing the principle of 'might is right' and thus perpetuating the order of the jungle. But when Arjuna sees that many of his old friends, close relatives and revered

[1] Sri Aurobindo, *On The Veda* (Pondicherry: Sri Aurobindo Ashram, 1956), p. 77.

[2] H. Zimmer, *Myths and Symbols in Indian Art and Civilization*, op. cit., pp. 3–11.

teachers happen to be in the opposing camp, he experiences a profound crisis of the spirit. His body begins to shake, his mouth goes dry, the bow slips from his hand, and his mind reels.[1] He then thinks that instead of fighting with friends and relatives it would be much better for him to retire into solitude and engage in peaceful contemplation of the Divine.

But the divine teacher Kṛṣṇa, the friend, philosopher and guide of Arjuna, administers him a sharp rebuke. He is quick to point out that Arjuna's sudden thought of ascetic retirement is a rationalization of his nervousness and his desire to escape from responsibility. The fundamental point at issue is not a personal matter concerning his longing for freedom or fondness for kinsmen. Whether he personally craves for the kingdom or not, whether he loves or hates his hostile kinsmen, is now beside the point. The crucial issue is a much larger ethical one affecting the very foundation of human society. It is the question of justice versus injustice, truth versus falsehood, the rule of law versus the rule of the jungle. To champion the cause of truth and justice is the unequivocal demand of the divine will operative in history. Not to perceive this divine significance of social and historical evolution amounts to spiritual blindness. So Kṛṣṇa explains that the highest religious duty for Arjuna would be to rise above all personal and emotional considerations and to make a definite choice in favour of the higher values of existence. To co-operate with the divine will in history, instead of renouncing life and society, is the unconditional imperative of spiritual insight.

Thus we find that the *Gītā* is most emphatic in presenting the dynamic spiritual ideal. Collective liberation consists in the evolution of society into the reign of truth. It consists not in simply realizing God but in co-operating with God towards the manifestation of the divine glory in the field of human relations and social action. Some kind of creative fellowship between man and God is an essential factor in this evolutionary consummation. Man has to make a definite choice in favour of truth, justice and progress, and act accordingly.

MODERN POLITICAL IDEOLOGIES

The epoch-making cultural event that happened at the beginning of contemporary western civilization was a nihilistic catharsis of the intellectual climate. Nietzsche announced 'God is dead' and made a clean sweep of religious pessimism, supernaturalism and asceticism. Life in this world was affirmed in its entirety, with its beauty and splendour and also its darkness and danger. Freedom of the individual self was recognized as the creative source of ever

[1] *The Bhagavadgītā*, I, 29 and 30.

new values. Marx declared that the course of history was determined not by God nor by transcendent ideas but by material forces and class conflicts in the economic sphere. Lenin condemned religion as the opium of the masses of the people. Freud sought to demonstrate that it was a grand illusion, a neurosis of the human race. They all felt convinced that the kingdom of heaven on earth, i.e. the collective liberation of mankind, would not descend from above but have to emerge from below. Leaders of the communist countries think that it has to be established on earth by means of revolutionary action on the part of the oppressed and downtrodden. Leaders of the democratic countries maintain that it would be conditional upon the acceptance of freedom as the central value of life. Genuine freedom alone can bring out the best in man—the best in different individuals, the best in different political groups, and the best in different nations of the world.

Revolutionary changes have taken place today in man's habits of thinking and ways of living. Rapid changes are still taking place all the time on account of ever new discoveries in science and technology. The international scene is dominated by the antagonism and power struggle between two superstates, the United States and Soviet Russia. They are the proponents of two mutually conflicting ideologies and value systems such as democracy and communism. Both of these ideologies have assumed a sort of religious complexion. They are addressed to the soul, that is, the value consciousness of man everywhere. Each of them promises to establish the kingdom of heaven on earth. Each of them is presented as the sovereign means of achieving the collective emancipation of mankind into the promised land of universal happiness, freedom and equality.

While the conflicting world ideologies of our present day promise the dawn of a new age of universal happiness, their mortal conflict is fraught with the dark danger of atomic annihilation. It represents the worst crisis in history. The colossal superpowers championing the two opposed ideologies are armed to the teeth with the most dangerous weapons of mass destruction. Their atomic might has reached the 'saturation'[1] point so that there is no longer any meaning of greater or lesser number of atomic bombs on this or that side. Any blunder anywhere in their elaborate push-button system of offence and defence may trigger an atomic holocaust of civilization. Each superpower has its own network of allies and satellites. There are all manner of pacts of non-aggression and mutual saftey linking up the small nations to the big powers. The foolish or neurotic plans of any mad little dictator in this vast network of political ties may

[1] John H. Herz, *International Politics in the Atomic Age* (New York: Columbia University Press, 1959), pp. 186–7.

suddenly start a global catastrophe. Thus the world sits on the edge of a volcano.

The supreme paradox of the present day world situation lies in this. When man has the most powerful means of self-defence and security, he suffers from the deepest sense of anxiety and insecurity. When he is most proud of his mastery over external nature, he is most afraid of his own image. This drives home to deeper thinking that material forces alone are inadequate to usher into existence a new heaven on earth. No amount of change in the externals of life, however helpful and important, is enough. No amount of mechanical perfection in the social, economical and political structure of collective living is enough. In ultimate analysis, it is the human factor—man behind the machine—which is of crucial importance. Everything ultimately depends upon the goodwill and genuine regard for human welfare on the part of the individuals who are invested with final political authority and placed in charge of the vast military apparatus. What is therefore of basic importance is a genuine change of heart, a radical transformation of consciousness, a spiritual reorientation of outlook, on the part of the powers that be. Most essentially needed is a total and dynamic insight into the identity of self-interest and world interest, a vivid realization of the indivisibility of human welfare.

A UNIFIED WORLD ORDER

Integral yoga envisages collective liberation as the emergence of a unique world order ruled by spiritual values. A spiritual world order would be the crowning fulfilment of the process of cosmic evolution. It would also be the unveiled manifestation of the glory of the spirit hidden in the heart of nature. It would be the consummation of evolutionary nature in spirit and the self-expression of spirit in the bosom of cosmic nature.

Prophets and mystics of the Middle Ages envisioned man's collective liberation either in terms of the supernatural (Judaeo-Christian) or in terms of pure transcendence (Hindu-Buddhist). The evolutionary significance of nature was not fully grasped. The dynamic presence of the power of transcendence was not always fully understood. The divine significance of destiny operative in history was not quite clearly comprehended. In consequence, a sharp distinction between nature and spirit was strongly emphasized. An attitude of world and life negation was frequently promoted.

Modern statesmen and political thinkers contemplate the establishment of a new age of peace and progress mainly in materialistic terms. Utmost reliance is placed on socio-political reforms and international pacts and agreements. Rising standards of living and improved machines and gadgets are often regarded as the great hope of mankind. It is frequently ignored that in the last analysis nothing is much availing if the soul of man remains unchanged. In the absence of an effective spiritual regeneration, all the glamour of materialistic civilization may prove utterly deceptive. It may presage the roving fires of death and destruction.

CHAPTER III

THE SYNTHESIS OF YOGAS: *HAṬHA, RĀJA, TANTRA* AND *JÑĀNA*

INTEGRAL Yoga represents the crowning fulfilment of the traditional yoga systems of India. It takes note of their limitations and one-sided tendencies. And it incorporates their inherent truths in a higher synthesis.

Broadly speaking, there are six traditional systems of yoga; *Haṭha, Rāja, Tantra, Jñāna, Bhakti* and *Karma*. Here a brief survey and critical evaluation will be made of the first four.

HAṬHA YOGA

Haṭhayoga is the system which starts with the body. Body and mind being closely interrelated, it aims at mastery over the body with a view to securing corresponding mastery over the mind. Control of nervous and vital energies produces control of mental functions. The mind-body complex being brought under perfect control, the indwelling spirit shines out and the higher self is realized.

Haṭha is derived from the roots, *ha* (sun) and *ṭha* (moon).[1] *Haṭha* is the equalization and stabilization of the 'sun breath' (i.e. the breath which flows through the right nostril) and the 'moon breath' (i.e. the breath which flows through the left nostril). *Haṭha* also means violence, force. Through the regulation of the physiological processes, *Haṭhayoga* forcibly releases the dormant energies of human personality.

The principal steps of *Haṭhayoga* are *āsana* and *prāṇāyāma*. *Āsana* consists of certain bodily postures such as lotus posture, hero posture, head stand, shoulder stand, etc. They are designed to stimulate the glands, vitalize the body, and strengthen the nervous system. Purified and strengthened nerves are the most important pre-requisite of yogic practice.

Prāṇāyāma means control of the vital energy through breath-regulation. It aims at mastery over the vital forces which are

[1] Theos Bernard, *Hatha Yoga* (New York: Columbia University Press, 1945), p. 1.

operative in the body. Through control of breath and mobilization of vital forces, it endeavours to secure the release and free flow of the fundamental psycho-physical energy (*kuṇḍalinī*) latent in the human system. This root energy being dynamized, the individual is set on the path leading to his reintegration with the ultimate ground of existence.

It is believed that one who acquires success in *Haṭhayoga* gains supernormal powers. He enjoys vibrant health, youthfulness and longevity. He attains spiritual liberation and supernal bliss.

The chief merit of *Haṭhayoga* lies in its insistence upon the basic importance of the body. Various bodily postures and breathing exercises recommended in *Haṭhayoga* are very effective means of developing the body as a fit and strong instrument of higher spiritual living. Mystics who have neglected the bodily factor, have suffered immensely on the physical plane. They have suffered from disease and disability, and have met with premature death. Profound spiritual experiences put an inordinate strain on the nervous system. They often come with the impact of a rushing flood. Without a prior bodily training and nervous firmness, many mystics fail to stand that impact. They are carried off by waves of emotion; they sing, dance, cry, and roll on the floor, failing to convert the flood of emotion into calm creative energy. *Haṭhayoga* can prepare and fortify one against this kind of mishap.

The chief defect of *Haṭhayoga* lies in its over-emphasis upon the physical side of existence. The body is sometimes almost deified. Preoccupation with the body produces excessive self-concern. Acquisition of supernormal powers and the bliss of personal salvation loom large on the mental horizon. An indifference to the affairs of the world and the requirements of society is generated. Not much interest is left for higher cultural pursuits. The need for intellectual development is not sufficiently recognized. The danger of going astray through selfish appropriation of whatever unusual power is gained is rampant. The spectacle of *Haṭhayogis* making a vain-glorious display in public of their extraordinary bodily control is not an uncommon sight. It is such misguided persons who have brought much disrepute upon the fair name of yoga.

RĀJA YOGA

Whereas *Haṭhayoga* starts with the body, *Rājayoga* starts with the mind. It works with the mental apparatus considered as a whole. It endeavours to achieve a complete cessation of all mental functions,[1] so that the light of the indwelling spirit may shine out. It recom-

[1] *The Yoga Sutras of Patanjali*, I, 1.

mends no doubt the methods of bodily posture (*āsana*) and breath-control (*prāṇāyāma*), but it does not require the practice of them in their full elaborateness as developed by *Haṭhayoga*. On the contrary it adapts them to its central purpose of mental calmness, balance and equilibrium. Of the numerous forms of bodily posture it specially selects that which keeps the body motionless in the fittest and most comfortable position helpful to the practice of breath-control and meditation. It recommends breathing exercises with a view to harmonizing the vital forces of the body, so that the obstructive elements of ignorance, inertia and restlessness may be removed.

Prior to the practice of bodily posture and breath-control, *Rājayoga* stresses the need for adequate ethico-religious training. The powers of body and mind are likely to be abused if the right spiritual foundation has not already been laid. The ethico-religious training recommended in *Rājayoga* consists of two steps: moral discipline (*yama*) and religious observances (*niyama*).

Moral discipline includes the practice of non-violence (*ahiṁsā*), truthfulness (*satya*), non-stealing (*asteya*), control of the sexual impulse (*brahmacarya*), and abstinence from greed or avariciousness involving non-acceptance of unnecessary gifts from those whose motives are questionable (*aparigraha*). Religious observances include the practice of internal and external purity (*sauca*), contentment implying the principle of plain living and high thinking (*santoṣa*), endurance of hardship and adverse circumstances (*tapas*), devoted study of spiritually ennobling books (*swādhyāya*) and self-surrender to the Divine (*Iśwara-praṇidhāna*).

The fifth important step in *Rājayoga* is self-withdrawal (*pratyāhāra*). It is the withdrawal of the senses from their external objects. It is the act of transcending the natural world. It should not be misconstrued as absolute and final world negation. It is the methodological device of temporarily setting aside the world with a view to inquiring with sustained energy into the nature of the spirit. It corresponds to what Edmund Husserl has called 'the phenomenological reduction'.[1] It is the method of putting into brackets the whole natural world, without paying any attention to the question whether the world is real or unreal and without using any 'judgement that concerns spatio-temporal existence'. The idea is to gain thereby full freedom and untrammelled energy in investigating the field of consciousness. When the question concerning the ontological status of the natural world is set aside, the contents and functions of consciousness can be observed in their essence as pure phenomena.

As an aspect of spiritual practice, *pratyāhāra* implies a shift in

[1] Edmund Husserl, *Ideas* (London: George Allen & Unwin Ltd., 1958,) pp. 110–11.

attention from the impulsive to the higher values of life. It signifies one's dissatisfaction with exclusive pre-occupation with material values or with the traditional and conventional mode of living. It involves what Plato has called 'divine discontent'. It involves a kind of 'metaphysical rebellion' against man's condition in the universe. *Pratyāhāra* is one's readiness to plunge into the unchartered sea of deeper self-inquiry and critical investigation into the meaning of life. It is the disengagement of the self from unthinking attachment to the not-self. It aims at transcending the world of false identifications and illusory projections in a deep search for the unconditioned spiritual reality.

In order to achieve the ultimate goal of freedom, *pratyāhāra* has to be supplemented by three other processes, namely, concentration (*dhāraṇā*) meditation (*dhyāna*) and self-integration (*samādhi*).

Concentration is the focusing of all mental energies upon one object, one central idea, or one relevant truth. It releases latent energies of the psyche and marshalls all psychic forces in a definite direction. Meditation is the higher phase of concentration. It is the free and uninterrupted flow of thought in one direction, centring round a definite theme. That theme may be the self, or pure existence, or the supreme value. It purifies the inner being, thoroughly cleanses the mental apparatus, and removes all unconscious obstructions to the unitary functioning of personality. It prepares the ground for self-integration or existential self-awareness (*samādhi*).

At first, existential self-awareness takes place on the mental level. This is called *savikalpa samādhi*. At this stage a person sees his own image reflected clearly and distinctly, as if on a flawless mirror or on the tranquil and transparent water of a pool. His purified mind, emancipated from the drive of desire and the taint of ignorance, is such a mirror. But still what is seen here is only an image of the self, the self known objectively, not the subjective reality of the self. So one has to advance still farther. At the next higher stage, the mental level is transcended. All mental functioning comes to a stop. The mirror or the pool disappears. A man now knows himself just by being his own true self. It is no more his image in a mirror that is seen, but his innermost reality. This is called *nirvikalpa samādhi*. This unobstructed and unmediated self-abiding is the essence of spiritual liberation according to *Rājayoga*.

Now, integral yoga fully appreciates the perfection of the technique which has been elaborately developed by *Rājayoga*. But it points out that the methods of *Rājayoga* are tailored to the concept of static realization of the self in its pure transcendence. They are not quite adequate for the purpose of dynamic self-identification with the Divine immanently operative in history. They are not quite suitable for man's intelligent co-operation with the creative force of cosmic evolution. For the fulfilment of the latter purpose, an active dedication from the very beginning to the cosmic purpose of existence is imperatively necessary. *Rājayoga* emphasizes the method of mental tranquillization as a means of attaining static self-realization. The danger of life negation, even though not a necessary sequel, is present in this approach. According to integral yoga, simultaneously with the processes of inward self-purification and mental serenity, active participation in life is essential. Social, cultural and humanitarian activities pursued in a spirit of self-offering to the Divine are an indispensable adjunct to the inward processes of concentration and meditation.

TĀNTRIC YOGA

Tāntric yoga is also known as *Kuṇḍalinī* or *Kuṇḍalī* yoga. It has some noteworthy characteristics of its own.

Tāntric yoga is closely connected with the worship of God as the supreme Mother. The Divine has two inseparable aspects: the archetypal masculine (Śiva), the archetypal feminine (Śakti). Śiva is pure Being, timeless perfection, eternal wisdom, logos. Śakti is the power of Becoming, the creative energy of time, the joy and love of self-expression, eros. Śakti is the Divine Mother who mediates between Being and the flux of becoming, between the Absolute and the sphere of relativity, between eternal perfection and the ceaseless flow of time. On the one hand Śakti is the medium of manifestation of the infinite in the finite. On the other hand she is the medium of self-fulfilment of the finite in the infinite. So the most natural approach for those who desire perfection is to seek the help, guidance and grace of the dynamic Divine.

The world as the manifestation of energy is an unceasing process, a perpetual flow. Our life is movement and action. But all movements, acts and processes ultimately flow from the universal creative energy, Śakti. This universal energy cannot be blind and unconscious. Nor is it conscious in the way in which the human mind is conscious. It is infinitely superior to human consciousness in depth of insight and breadth of vision. Having created the human individual, Śakti enters into him and dwells within him as his main support and centre of gravity. This dynamic nucleus, the central psycho-physical power latent in man, is called *Kuṇḍalinī*, the coiled power (the serpent energy). The serpent while resting stays in coiled form, and while moving and acting it uncoils itself. Similarly, the creative energy has its dormant and dynamic, static and kinetic aspects. Different vital functions such as respiration, digestion, procreation, elimination, etc. are different modes of operation of the *Kuṇḍalinī*. Different mental functions such as perception, reflection, emotion, volition, etc. are also modes of manifestation of the *Kuṇḍalinī*. Science teaches us that in the structure of an atom, there are electrons or negative charges of electricity which move round a positive nucleus which is apparently static. Likewise, in the human organism there are numerous vital and mental functions which are centrally supported by the positive nucleus of the *Kuṇḍalinī*.

Tāntric yoga is the art of splitting the spiritual atom in man. It is the technique of releasing the pent-up energies of the human psyche. When the *Kuṇḍalinī* is dynamized, the individual experiences a tremendous upsurge of energy from within. He feels it as the power of God working within him. He feels that he is being guided from within, with infinite patience and love, by the Divine Mother. A re-orientation of his outlook towards spiritual values takes place. A deep longing for the eternal leaps into flame. New vistas of thought are opened. Centres of extra-sensory perception are stimulated. The search for the ultimate is intensified.

According to *Tāntric* yoga true spiritual development begins with the awakening of the *Kuṇḍalinī*. Prior to this awakening, all ethical and religious practices are in the nature of self-preparation. They purify the heart of the individual and direct his attention to the spiritual destiny of life. After the *Kuṇḍalinī* is awakened, spiritual growth seems to be guided no more by the ego but by a deeper power within. Meditation becomes in a sense effortless and spontaneous. A process of deepening self-awareness and joyful self-expansion sets in. Unconscious motivations are gradually brought to light, and a genuine spirit of dedication to the Divine begins to permeate the whole being.

According to *Tāntric* yoga, the ultimate goal of spiritual effort is the union of the dynamic and static aspects of personality. We have noted that Tantra affirms the reality of God as the unity of timeless perfection (Śiva) and the dynamism of time (Śakti). Man who is an image of God is also essentially the unity of the power of becoming and the perfection of being. Through social, cultural, ethical and religious activities, man prepares himself for the fulfilment of his spiritual destiny. The practice of yoga, which involves self-energizing and self-transcending, advances him to a higher phase of spiritual growth. This process of growth is carried to perfection when the timeless dimension of existence is discovered. In *Kuṇḍalinī* yoga union with the timeless is believed to be total and complete. It is not simply union through the intellect or the heart. It is a kind of total psycho-physical union. It is the union of one's total self-energy with the timeless ground of being. Symbolically, it is represented as a sort of mystic marriage (*mahāmaithuna*) between the feminine and the masculine aspects of personality—between the principles of basic energy and pure existence. A flood of delight is released from this mystic union. On all the levels of body and mind indescribable waves of joy are experienced.

Tāntric yoga is boldly affirmative in its methodological approach. Other yoga systems have laid much stress upon renunciation and desirelessness as essential aids to liberation. But *Tāntric* yoga affirms the need for intelligent and organized fulfilment of natural desires. In its view there is no basic antagonism between nature and spirit. Nature is the creative power of spirit in the objective sphere. Nobody therefore can enter the kingdom of spirit without first obtaining a passport from nature. Practice of austerity, asceticism and self-mortification is an insult to nature. It creates more difficulties than it can solve. By weakening the body and producing inner conflicts and tensions, it undermines balanced and healthy development. It is only by following the spirit of nature that one can swim with the current and capture the kingdom of heaven by storm.

Worship of the Divine Mother implies appreciation of the presence of profound wisdom in nature, both external and internal. There is a principle of cosmic intelligence operative in external nature. It controls the process of cosmic evolution. Similarly, there is deep wisdom inherent in man's inner nature, in his unconscious psyche. It secretly determines his inner evolution. If a person intelligently follows the bent of his own nature, his desires become more and more refined and lofty. Base desires gradually yield place to noble desires. Lower impulses are replaced by higher impulses. When a child's natural desire to play with toys is duly satisfied, it is soon outgrown yielding place to a keen interest in books or living playmates. When a man's natural desire for sex is lawfully satisfied, it gives rise to a growing interest in social welfare or humanitarian service. When his desire for enjoying the world is duly satisfied on the basis of intelligent self-organization, one day it gives rise to a deeper longing for Transcendence.

So *Tāntric* yoga prescribes what is called desireful prayer and worship (*sakāma upāsanā*). All natural desires are accepted as modes of manifestation of the creative spirit of nature. The problem is to organize them intelligently with a view to the maximum satisfaction and fulfilment of one's nature. There is divine sanction behind such self-fulfilment. One can also invoke divine blessings in such self-fulfilment. One places one's desires before God, and then, with God's sanction and sanctification, proceeds to fulfil them in a spirit of self-offering to the Divine. This brings about an increasing refinement and spiritual transformation of one's desire-nature. A constructive channelling of the libido towards the higher ends of existence takes place.

Tantra believes in the principle of 'like cures like'. When a person suffers from water in his ears, the doctor injects more water into his ear drums so that all the accumulated water comes out. When a person gets sick on account of a certain kind of poison inside his body, the doctor may prescribe for him the same kind of poison to be taken in the right dose in medicinal form. When a person falls down to the ground, it is with the support of the ground that he jumps to his feet again. Similarly, it is with the help of passion that the problem of passion can be solved. Sensuous desires and personal ambitions are usually condemned as impediments to spiritual progress. Cravings for delicacies, for sex, for stimulants, etc., as well as longings for wealth, social position, political power, etc., are often regarded by religion as temptations of the devil. But *Tantra* says: 'All these desires ultimately come from the divine will. In the final analysis they are aids to the process of evolution and progress. The important thing is to fulfil them with that understanding in a spirit of co-operation with the creative force of evolution. The creative force of evolution is no other than the divine will immanent in the world process. The more a person co-operates with the evolutionary impetus, the more his desires are purged of the egotistic taint and are transmuted into the pure flame of aspiration for divine life.' This is the underlying truth of the *Tāntric* theory of the five M's.[1] Such ingredients as wine (*Madya*), meat (*Māṁsa*), fish (*Matsya*), parched cereal (*Mudrā*), and sexual union (*Maithuna*) are considered valuable aids to vigorous growth and development. They represent different modes of manifestation of energy. Those who can make profitable use of them, in union with the supreme creative power, towards the ends of harmonious self-development and social progress, belong to the heroic type of yogi.

It may be observed here that the affirmative approach of *Tāntric* yoga contains a precious element of truth. It is a protest against the extreme tendencies of asceticism, self-mortification, world and life negation, etc. It affirms nature as the dynamism of spirit. It affirms life as the diversified expression of transcendence. But it has often the tendency to carry the spirit of affirmation too far. Over-emphasis upon life affirmation may prove as misleading as over emphasis upon ascetic renunciation. The balanced spiritual ideal lies midway between these two extremes. When people develop a strong ascetic tendency, it is necessary to tell them about the positive significance of life, nature and society. On the other hand, when people become

[1] Sir John Woodroffe, *Shakti and Shakta* (Madras: Ganesh & Co., 1959), pp. 578–9.

too affirmative in following the way of nature, it is desirable to tell them about the transcendent glory of the spirit. Otherwise, one may get lost in the labyrinth of desire and practise self-deception in the name of religion. That is why we find that a huge amount of malpractice came in course of time to be associated with *Tāntric* yoga. Sexual promiscuity is sometimes sanctioned as a mode of concerted power worship. Black magic puts on the religious mask. Ruthless slaughter of animals is approved as symbolic self-sacrifice to God.

Even though *Tāntric* yoga is affirmative in its method and approach, it differs little from asceticism with regard to the ultimate goal of spiritual effort. The *Tāntric* method of life affirmation is also designed oftener than not to statically blissful union with the formless consciousness of the eternal. It has been said: 'When Kundali "sleeps" man is awake to this world. When she "awakes" he sleeps, that is, loses all consciousness of the world and enters his causal body. In Yoga he passes beyond to formless Consciousness.'[1] Thus here again we come across the ideal of static and transcendent realization inherent in traditional mysticism. At this point integral yoga wishes to remind us emphatically that static and formless consciousness is not the ultimate goal. The formless nontemporal is only one aspect of Being. The evolving world of endless forms is another no less important aspect of Being. Our goal is to join forces with the evolution of higher forms and values in union with the formless depth of Being.

The concept of total union with the eternal is a very significant contribution of *Tantra*. We have to be integrated with Being not only by way of contemplation or devotion or love. Our entire existence including the physical and the unconscious has to be lifted up to the thrilling touch of the eternal. The conscious and unconscious aspects of our being have to be unified. The static and dynamic aspects of our personality have to be harmonized. But this notion of total union could not be developed in *Tantra* to its furthest logical sequel on account of limitations imposed by medieval metaphysics. Medieval metaphysics conceived of the inmost essence of Being in terms of transcendence and eternity. It had no adequate comprehension of the ontological significance of evolution and history.

In conformity with the metaphysical outlook of the age, total union is envisaged in *Tantra* as the union of a man's entire personality with formless eternity. The central psycho-physical energy (*Kuṇḍalī*) is awakened so that with his whole being the yogi may experience the transcendent bliss of the absolute, having completely withdrawn himself from the world of form and change. Now, strictly speaking, this is not total union in the full sense of the term. The

[1] Sir John Woodroffe, *Shakti and Shakta*, op. cit., p. 673.

eternal is incomplete without the historical. Perfection is incomplete without evolution. The creative flow of time is an essential factor in the structure of eternity. So total union must imply that while we are anchored in the timeless foundation of Being, we have to act in our historical situations as dynamic centres of Being. The ultimate purpose of the transformation of our physical and vital nature is to prepare us for the supreme task of life. That task is to establish higher values in society and to manifest the glories of eternity in time.

Thus in integral yoga the notion of total union develops into integral union. It is the union of the total self with total reality. It implies union with the creative force of evolution as well as union with the immutable joy of eternity. Contact with the eternal brings supreme wisdom and joy and love into our being. But wisdom, joy and love cannot be divorced from action. To know God is to love God. To love God is to serve God. To glimpse the will of God is to act for the glory of God in the world. Such action is co-operation with the creative force of evolution, because the latter is another name for the will of God operative in the world process. Enlightened action is indeed of the very essence of human reality. Through such action we joyfully participate in the movement of time, anchored in the serenity of the timeless. So it may be stated that integral union is the union of wisdom, love and action. It is union with history as well as with transcendence.

THE PATH OF KNOWLEDGE ('JÑĀNA YOGA')

The point of departure on the path of knowledge is the will to know inherent in the human mind. The longing for truth is universal. Man is equipped with intellectual faculties needed for the comprehension of truth. But there are some in whom the intellectual quest of truth is the dominant interest in life. The path of knowledge is particularly suitable for them.

There are seven essential steps or limbs of the path of knowledge. These are: discrimination (*viveka*), detachment (*vairāgya*), self-discipline (*tapasyā*), longing for freedom (*mumukṣutā*), hearing (*śravaṇa*), reflection (*manana*) and meditation (*nididhyāsana*).

Discrimination means clear understanding of the distinction between the real and the unreal, between the permanent and the transient. It is a grasp of the distinction between truth and falsehood, and between the self and the not-self. All human suffering is ultimately traceable to our estrangement from the self, the inmost centre of existence. Self-estrangement leads to false identification with things which are foreign to the self. It makes one run after shadows, the passing and perishing things of life, like a child chasing colourful butterflies.

Discrimination leads to detachment or withdrawal from the ephemeral values of life. It is a kind of awakening from materialistic slumber. The futility of sensuous enjoyments is clearly perceived. The vanity and self-devouring quality of the search for material possessions is revealed. All craving for sensuous objects of enjoyment either in this world or in a supernatural heaven is given up. A man who is plunged in the immediacy of pleasure-seeking and pleasure-expecting is not yet ready for the spiritual quest of truth. He is too much attached to the world to be able to inquire into the ultimate meaning of the world. A breach with immediacy is an essential condition of the spiritual quest. Detachment is this breach with immediacy.

Self-discipline involves six factors: calmness (*śama*), restraint (*dama*), renunciation (*uparati*), forbearance (*titikṣā*), faith (*śraddhā*), and self-settledness (*samādhāna*).

Our mind acts like a monkey jumping from branch to branch on the tree of life in search of different fruits. Calmness (*sama*) is the act of overcoming this restlessness of the mind. In attaining this calmness, intellectual understanding of the futility of sensuous enjoyments is not enough. It has to be reinforced by assiduous tutoring of the unconscious mind.

The task of maintaining calmness is not an easy job. It is occasionally threatened by distractions, allurements, outside noises and suggestions, etc. One must develop the ability to protect oneself against such disquieting factors. This is called restraint (*dama*). It is the restraining of the external sense organs.

In one's search for the spiritual truth all kinds of attachment have to be left behind. Emotional ties to parents, spouse, children, kith and kin, etc. have to be transcended. Fondness for conventional rituals and ceremonies has to be outgrown. Blind conformity to fixed social norms and customs and traditional patterns has to be abandoned. This act of shaking loose from all bonds of emotion and convention is called cessation or renunciation (*uparati*).

The spiritual path is not strewn with roses. A sacrifice of creature comforts has to be made. Much hardship has to be endured. One must get used to the extremes of changing weather and the strains of rugged living. One should not be carried off by praise and adoration nor adversely affected by blame and criticism. One should develop the inner strength to face all worries and anxieties and endure inner conflicts. This is called forbearance (*titikṣā*).

In spite of all courage and perseverance, there are bound to be moments of darkness, doubt and despair. Self-confidence is sometimes badly shaken. The inner vision gets clouded. There are sinister suggestions to the effect that the spiritual goal is after all a chimera, a phantom of the imagination. In these moments of darkness, the power of faith (*śraddhā*) alone can sustain. It is faith in the sayings and shining examples of illumined teachers. It is faith in the testimony of the great books of wisdom.

As doubts and distractions are eliminated, the seeker concentrates with growing conviction upon the ultimate goal. His conviction is not merely intellectual assent but affirmation of his total self. With the single-minded devotion of his entire being, he now settles down to the consummation of his spiritual task. This is self-settledness (*samādhāna*).

The course of self-discipline as stated above thoroughly purifies a person and produces in him a genuine aspiration for truth and freedom. At the beginning, when a person turns to spiritual life, he may be prompted by mixed motivations. Along with his spiritual seeking there may be a hidden desire for recognition and renown. There may be an unconscious will to power, a will to surpass rivals and to conquer the world. There may be a secret wish to achieve something big by following a short cut, or by discovering some kind of a magic wand. But out of a long process of self-discipline is born that pure flame of spiritual longing which aims at freedom and freedom alone. This is called *mumukṣutā.*

At this point the seeker is ready to be introduced to the supreme truth. Now, in Hindu philosophy the essential truth has always been regarded as beyond all verbalized expression. Propositional form is simply inadequate to its content. The essence of truth is a matter of inward realization. It is a matter of immediate experience on a silent, non-verbal level.

The potentiality of such immediate experience is present in all. A man of supreme enlightenment has the power of awakening the spiritual potential in others. He can function as a spiritual guide or guru. When a person has a genuine longing for freedom, he must proceed to find out an authentic guru. The guru, in recognition of the disciple's readiness, communicates to him the supreme truth. In Vedānta the highest truth relates to the identity of the spirit in man and the supreme Being (*ātman* is *Brahman*). The teacher says to the disciple, 'That Thou art'. The disciple hears it with all the receptivity of his purified consciousness. This is called *śravaṇa,* hearing. No mere verbal communication is this. It is symbolical of an existential contact between two complementary souls. A direct transmission of power takes place. The vision of truth which was slumbering in the disciple is struck into flame.

The next step is systematic reflection (*manana*). When a profound truth is born in the mind, the surrounding forces of darkness rush to devour it. Fresh doubts crop up. Contrary suggestions present themselves. All manner of contradictions appear. So the seeker has now to embark upon an arduous process of sustained thinking. Doubts and contradictions have to be patiently dissolved with the help of the teacher. Various ideas have to be organized into a self-coherent whole. Reason is allowed to play its rightful function in the complete assimilation of truth.

The next step, the seventh important phase, of the path of knowledge, is meditation (*nididhyāsana*). Meditation has the power of transforming intellectual understanding into non-dual realization, philosophic knowledge into spiritual wisdom proper. The intellect is incurably dualistic. To the eye of philosophic contemplation, the self or Being is after all an object of thinking, however absolute and comprehensive that object may be postulated to be. The intellect cannot bridge the gulf between subject and object. What is ordinarily known as intuition is also not free from the dualism of knower and known, even though the relation between them is perceived here as direct. It is only by means of meditation that the dualism of intellect and intuition is wholly transcended. Meditation leads to that transcendental awareness in which subject, object and their cognitive relation are existentially unified. Attainment of transcendental awareness is known as *nirvikalpa samādhi*, the non-dual identity consciousness. It is the discovery of that fourth dimension of existence (*tūrīya*)[1] which is beyond space-time and also beyond cause-effect. It represents the ultimate goal and final phase of the path of knowledge. Having attained this pure non-dual consciousness, an individual realizes full freedom and conquers all fear, anxiety, doubt and despair.

The yoga of knowledge is unsurpassed in depth of spiritual insight in the history of man's religious experience. Its concept of non-dual identity-consciousness represents the loftiest summit of mystic realization. It shows how by following the intellectual bent of our nature, we can eventually attain existential realization of the supreme truth.

But the yoga of knowledge as it was developed in the dialectic of Śaṅkara and his followers in the medieval period suffers from some limitations which must be overcome. It considers the renunciation of society and human relations as an essential condition of enlightenment. The monastic ideal is over-emphasized; life in the monastery is eulogized as the highest mode of spiritual existence. This encourages young spiritual seekers to develop a spirit of world and life negation.

[1] Swami Nikhilananda, *The Upanishads*, Vol. 2 (New York: Harper & Brothers, 1952), pp. 236–8.

On account of an over-emphasis upon the intellectual side of human nature, the volitional and emotional aspects of personality are not duly recognized. A follower of the path of knowledge is often faced with the danger of being unconsciously affected by the characteristic aloofness of the intellect—aloofness from the affairs of the world, from the weal and woe of mankind, from the problems of man's material and social existence.

Intellectual aloofness is further re-inforced by a sense of spiritual alienation from the world. Asceticism involves withdrawal of the libido from the world. It brings about a resulting devaluation and deprecation of the world. Such world deprecation is then sought to be justified by the theory that the world is unreal from the standpoint of the absolute. Having realized the absolute, the liberated person goes through life mechanically in a spirit of supreme indifference. His teaching has the effect of inspiring the same negativism and indifference in others. This ascetic approach contributed in no small measure to the backwardness of India in matters of social reconstruction, economical advancement and political organization. So at the beginning of the modern era, the great Indian poet Rabindranath Tagore unambiguously denounced the ascetic ideal of life. He said, 'Deliverance is not for me in renunciation. I feel the embrace of freedom in a thousand bonds of delight'.[1] He stressed the concept of freedom in the midst of countless bonds of society and human relationship. Indian renaissance began with an affirmative and dynamic attitude to life. It began with an optimistic gospel of social reconstruction, political freedom, and cultural creativity.

[1] Rabindranath Tagore, *Gitanjali* (London: Macmillan & Co., 1949), p. 68.

CHAPTER IV

THE SYNTHESIS OF YOGAS: *BHAKTI*, *KARMA* AND *PŪRṆA*

THE YOGA OF LOVE (BHAKTI)

THE yoga of love starts with the natural feelings and emotions of the human heart. Love of the self, the desire to serve the beloved, love of playmates, affection for parents and children, and love of the spouse, are the most fundamental modes of human emotion. The technique of the yoga of love consists in turning them more and more to God, the ultimate ground of existence. An increasing spiritual orientation of natural emotions is the secret here.

Love of one's own self is the most elemental emotion in man. The instinct of self-preservation, the search for liberty, security and happiness, the longing for recognition and renown, are the different forms of manifestation of elemental self-love. The yoga of love shows how through a proper tutoring and deepening of one's basic sense of self-interest, the energy of self-love can be directed to the Divine. The Divine is not only the creator and loving preserver of all existence. The Divine is also one's true inmost Self, the all-controlling higher Self. The orientation of self-love to God is called *Śānta*.

The spirit of service (*sevā*) is an essential component of love. Rooted in the heart of every man is a strong desire to render loving service to the benefactor, to the well-wisher, to the protector and provider. Sacrifices are gladly made to please him. The yoga of love seeks to turn this spirit of service and self-sacrifice to God who is the ultimate protector and provider for all living creatures. This is the usual pattern in all popular religions. A pious man takes refuge in God as the sovereign master and ruler of the universe. He looks upon himself as an humble servant of God, the supreme lord of the world. He experiences perfect security and happiness in the service of the Divine. This is called *Dāsya*.

Then there is the natural longing for companionship and friendship. This longing can be turned to God. God may be regarded as man's unfailing friend and ever-present companion. Even in his absolute loneliness, he need not be afraid nor feel helpless. Even when the whole world deserts him, he may count upon God as his eternal friend, philosopher and guide. Such a spiritual orientation of the need for friendship is called *Sakhya.*

Then there is the sweet love-relationship between parent and child. Such a love relationship can easily be established between man and the supreme ruling power of the universe. The cosmic ruler may be regarded as the heavenly Father or the heavenly Mother, according to the strongest emotional need of the individual. In doing so one's devotion to father or mother is religiously sublimated. It brings happiness, peace and security to the individual and makes his life profoundly meaningful. In a matriarchal society it is natural to conceive of God as the cosmic Mother. In a patriarchal society it is natural to think of God as the heavenly Father. In a country like India where matriarchal and patriarchal societies have flourished for long side by side, mutually influencing each other, the cosmic principle comes to be regarded as the heavenly Father-Mother, with an equal accent upon both aspects. So the Divine in Hindu philosophy is Śiva-Śakti, Iśwara-Māyā, Rādhā-Kṛṣṇa, Rām-Sītā, etc. God is the integral unity of the archetypal masculine and feminine principles.

Then again there is a natural affection in the human heart for children. Love of children is universal. It can be religiously transformed. One can turn to God as the eternal child, embodying simplicity, spontaneity, freshness, joy, freedom and truth. One can also be devoted to the service of children as pure manifestations of the Divine. The archetypal image of the divine child is to be found in most of the religions and mythologies of the world. Mystics long for the divine child to be born in their inner consciousness. The birth of the divine child in man symbolizes the bursting of the light of truth in the human mind or the emergence of a spiritually transfigured personality. The concept of divine incarnation (*avatāra*)—the spirit made flesh—plays a significant part in providing religious orientation to man's deep love and longing for the child. When God is believed to be manifested on earth as a child, like baby Kṛṣṇa or baby Jesus, man has an opportunity of lavishing his affections upon God revealed as the Son of Man. This is called *vātsalya bhāva.*

Finally, there is the strongest of all instinctual-emotional drives in human nature, namely, the erotic impulse. All other emotions may get swallowed up in it. All other feelings and impulses may be constellated round the erotic impulse as their nucleus. It is well known that complete satisfaction in this world of the erotic impulse is extremely rare, if not impossible. Passion in man is insatiable. Hence the vast importance of religious sublimation. Without some spiritual orientation of elemental human emotions, the restlessness of the human spirit can become terribly devastating. Religious orientation of the erotic impulse is known as *madhura bhāva.*

The yoga of love involves spiritual transformation of the erotic impulse. A religious seeker, whether male or female, may look upon himself as a bride in relation to God. From the spiritual standpoint, God is the one supreme Bridegroom, the universal lover. The goal of religious effort is a kind of mystic marriage (*saṅgama* or *sammilana*) between the human soul and the universal spirit. The proper religious attitude of the soul is one of utter submission, total and unconditional surrender to the divine will. Many mystics in different parts of the world have approached God in this attitude.

But in the structure of our love there is a desire to take as well as a desire to give. There is an active attitude of acquisition and appropriation as well as a passive attitude of submission and sacrifice. In both males and females these two impulses are interwoven in various proportions. So we find that in the case of some mystics along with the spirit of devotion there is a dominant note of appropriation. God is regarded as honey, an ocean of honey; the human soul gains supreme blessedness through enjoyment of the celestial honey. Or, God is regarded as a treasure, the richest treasure of the world. The religious task is to find out that treasure and benefit from it. Or, God is a kingdom, the beatific kingdom of heaven. The spiritual destiny of life is to enter into the kingdom of heaven. Some wish to capture the kingdom of heaven by storm or with 'love's flashing sword'. Here the masculine component of love is in evidence. Sir Mohammed Iqbal says that life is an assimilative activity and that it assimilates even God. 'The Fountain of Life is Love's flashing sword.'[1]

Common to all these concepts of love-relationship between man and God is an abiding faith in the personality of God. God is conceived as the supreme Person who is capable of entering into an intimate relationship with man. He can respond to man's prayer and worship, love and devotion. Theistic mysticism the world over, whether Śaiva, or Vaiṣṇava, or Sufi or Christian, affirms the reality of personal God. It also affirms the possibility of man's direct union and loving communion with the Divine.

Traditional theism, whether Jewish or Christian or Islamic, has fought shy of the notion of man's direct union with the Divine. It stresses the need for a mediator—a prophet (Moses) or a messiah (Christ) or a divine messenger (Mohammed). God who is personal is infinite, absolute, transcendent and eternally perfect. So it is impossible for finite, imperfect and sinful man to enter into direct union with the absolute spirit. Man's salvation lies in atonement and

[1] Sir Mohammed Iqbal, *The Secrets of the Self*, pp. 73, 89.

reconciliation. When man sincerely repents for his sins, makes penance for them, turns to God with absolute submission, and accepts His chosen representative, he receives the grace of God and is saved. Soren Kierkegaard has called it Repetition. When man learns how to exist before God and accepts His inscrutable manifestation in the Son of Man, he receives His saving grace. When he loses everything before God and yet keeps his faith alive, he gets back everything double.[1] This is no direct union with God, but the reception of divine blessings through faith and surrender, through acceptance of the absurd (i.e. the christological dogma of the Spirit made flesh).

Devotional mysticism holds that man can enter into direct union with God because of the spiritual kinship between them. If God is like the Cosmic Flame, the finite soul is like a spark of fire. If God is like an ocean, the finite soul is like a river flowing into the ocean. Since God is absolute love, as soon as the obstacles of ignorance separating man from God are removed, the magnetic pull of divine love irresistibly attracts man into immediate contact with the Divine. The prophet or messiah is a visible manifestation of divine love. He provides a concrete focal point for the religious emotions of the human heart. By doing so his chief function is to guide the human soul ultimately into the immediate presence of the Divine. His purpose is not simply to save mankind from sinfulness, and to effectuate reconciliation through repentance and faith. This is certainly true for the masses up to a certain point of their spiritual growth. But the messiah has a still higher purpose. That purpose is to save mankind from ignorance and blind dogmas and absurd creeds. The divine personality is born in the world in order to show mankind the way beyond intellect and emotion and faith to direct union with the infinite.

The Vaiṣṇava mystics of India have envisaged man's direct encounter with the Divine in various ways. It may assume the form of perpetual living in the blissful presence of God (*sāmīpya*). It may assume the form of life everlasting on the same plane of consciousness with God (*sālokya*). It may consist in transformation into a perfect image of the Divine through His gracious touch (*sārūpya*). It may be attainment of the same law of action as that of God (*sādharmya*). It may consist in acquiring supernatural powers in order to function as an effective instrument of God (*sārṣṭi*). It may be the realization of oneness of being by entering into the celestial body of God (*sāyujya*). Finally, it may be a state of selfless service and self-offering at the feet of God in utter disregard of one's personal liberation and happiness (*sevā*). Whatever the specific ideal and

[1] Soren Kierkegaard, *Repetition* (Princeton: Princeton University Press, 1946), p. 132.

aspiration of a particular seeker may be, the grace of God is the indispensable condition of his spiritual fulfilment. Love and love alone—unmotivated and unconditional love—makes one fit for the grace of God. Knowledge and action are subordinate to love. They are instrumental to its full flowering.

Be it observed here that the idea of the religious growth of personality out of its own natural roots is very profound and effective. One has to start from where one is. One has to begin with those impulses and emotions which are deep-seated in one's nature. The concept of Personal God is without doubt of inestimable importance in the spiritual orientation and constructive channelling of human emotions. But complete spiritual maturity demands that one ultimately outgrows the bounds of emotionalism and personalism.

For the average person it is indeed immensely helpful to think of God as heavenly Father or cosmic Mother or Mystic Bridegroom. These are potent archetypal images embedded in the structure of the human psyche. But beyond a certain point of psychic growth, one has to grasp their character as inadequate symbols. The Divine is essentially neither father nor mother, neither male nor female, neither bridegroom nor bride. Nor can the Divine be partial or emotionally attached to any particular tribe or race or religious group. All races, nations and peoples are equal in the eyes of God. Nobody has a monopoly on the supreme truth. And the idea of divine favouritism is the product of human ambition and will to power. So in the course of religious development one has finally to outgrow all anthropomorphic images and comprehend the essence of God as indeterminable Being, as ineffable Superconsciousness.

In the integral growth of personality it is imperatively necessary that one appreciates the value of a religious symbol without exalting it to the rank of the absolute. We can certainly recognize the importance of a symbol without identifying it with the symbolized. Religious devotion frequently produces emotional fixation upon a determinate symbol of the absolute. This symbol may be a scripture, a creed, a leader, a church, or a mission. It reveals the absolute in a definite sphere of the relative. It affords us a glimpse of the absolute and yet is endowed with only relative validity. An understanding of this can help us to combine breadth of vision with depth of emotion. For instance, we can fully appreciate the extraordinary greatness and holiness of a religious leader. But that need not prompt us to repudiate or deprecate the outstanding merits of other great religious leaders. Likewise, we may dedicate ourselves heart and soul to a specific religious mission or creed. But that need not prevent our broad-minded appreciation of other valuable missions and creeds in the world.

The concept of a Personal God is indeed the highest religious symbol. It symbolizes the aspect of Being as cosmic creative energy. It implies that cosmic creativity is no blind mechanical force but is in the nature of cosmic intelligence. It further implies that the cosmic principle has an abiding interest in its diversified creation and individualized self-expressions. It is not indifferent to the values that emerge in the course of evolution. But that need not prompt us to identify a determinate theological conception of Personal God with the absolute.

Different theological conceptions of God—Christian, Islamic, Hindu, Buddhist, etc.—are necessarily limited and relatively valid perspectives of the cosmic creative principle. The cosmic reality can be called personal in so far as it is a profound creative intelligence, even though radially different in structure from the human intellect. It is also personal in so far as it seems to care for the production and conservation of higher values. But it is certainly not personal in the sense that it is partial to any particular race or nation or religious group. Like the sun it shines equally upon all peoples. Nor is it personal in the sense that it can be exclusively identified with any particular historical figure such as Jesus or Gautama or Kṛṣṇa. They are all historical manifestations of one evolutionary world-spirit. Each appeared on the historical stage to fulfil a particular mission. Each made an impact upon history towards the further advancement of mankind. But with the change of circumstances the teaching of each of them had to be considerably modified. No verbal teaching can indeed be equated with the absolute truth. So, none of the world teachers can be said to have uttered the last word of wisdom. Every one of them has to be understood and appreciated with reference to the historical context in which he taught. To raise such a question as: 'Who among the various religious leaders of history is higher and who the highest?', betrays an infantile attitude of the mind.

Religious devotion often assumes the form of undivided allegiance to a particular religious leader. Such undivided allegiance has without doubt much value in one's spiritual growth. It channels energy in a definite direction. It promotes sustained endeavour towards the fulfilment of one's chosen ideal of life. But such devotion or allegiance need not prompt one to downgrade other religious teachers. To do so is infantilism. It begets religious parochialism. It hinders the unfolding of a cosmic vision of the truth. Therein lies the great danger of a purely devotional approach. Until and unless devotion is consummated in authentic spiritual enlightenment, the danger is always there. Spiritual enlightenment, variously designated as *bodhi*, *prajñā*, *nirvāṇa*, *satori*, cosmic consciousness, etc., is a radically different dimension of experience beyond the intellectual and emotional functions of the mind. It is reflected on the mental level as the harmony of love and wisdom.

Another danger inherent in the purely devotional approach is the undermining of practical efficiency. The more a person allows himself to be carried off by waves of emotion, ecstasy and rapture, the more incapacitated he becomes in the practical field. He shouts and sings in joy, he rolls on the floor, he dances in a mood of frenzy. He sweats and trembles, and he may repeatedly fall into swoons. All such emotional agitation or holy-rollerism pretty soon brings about nervous exhaustion.

In the interest of the integration of personality it is desirable that the influx of emotion occasioned by spiritual practice should be turned into calm creative energy. The intensified devotion, the exuberance of love and joy, has to be properly channelled under the guidance of some socioethical, or humanitarian or culturally creative purpose of existence. Emotion is energy. But energy needs to be informed with a definite practical end in order to be productive. Intelligence has to impart serenity to emotion in order that it may bear fruit in creative action. A strengthening of the will to do is an essential supplement to the desire for love and joy.

THE YOGA OF ACTION (KARMA)

The yoga of action lays stress upon the volitional side of human nature. It regards the will to live, the striving for growth and perfection, as the natural starting-point for spiritual training. Action is indeed of the very essence of life. No man can ever stop acting. The question is whether he is engaged in some fruitful action or in meaningless action. The inescapable need for action is reflected in the popular saying: 'An idle man's brain is the devil's workshop.'

When a person withdraws from the outside world and shuts himself up in his solitary room, he is still acting. His action may assume the form of uncontrolled day-dreaming or free floating on the clouds of fancy. Or, it may assume the form of detached contemplation of past experiences or methodical self-inquiry. Or, he may find himself with an empty mind ringing with the jarring voices of unwelcome guests from the tombs of the unconscious. Even when a person goes to the hills, he may carry the whole of society upon his shoulders. His unfulfilled desires and repressed wishes are sure to accompany him everywhere. He withdraws from all purposive action only to find his mental vacuum filled with the ineffectual self-paintings of the repressed libido.

So the yoga of action seeks to solve the basic problem of man on the basis of properly guided action. It is particularly suitable for those who are men of active habits. It tries to regulate one's life of action in such a way that spiritual freedom and self-fulfilment can be attained through a re-fashioning of the whole business of living.

Now, what is action (karma)? And what is the standard of ideal spiritual action? Broadly speaking, there are three concepts of ideal spiritual action. Accordingly, the yoga of action may be understood in three different ways.

First of all, spiritual action may mean the performance of religious rites and ceremonies as recommended in such holy scriptures as the Vedas. Scriptural injunction is the ultimate standard of spiritual action. Whether scriptural injunction reflects eternal impersonal laws or the will of God conceived as the essence of law, is a controversial issue into which we need not enter here. The point to be noted is that conformity to scriptural injunction is the foundation of religious ethics.

Pious men engage in religious rites and offer sacrifices to various deities. They also perform various acts of charity such as rewarding the holy, feeding the hungry, clothing the naked, providing shelter to the homeless, and the like. But such acts of charity may not be motivated by pure compassion or love of man. Above everything else, they are an essential ingredient of the scrupulous performance of sacrificial ceremonies. The dominant motive is conformity to scriptural injunction or to ethico-religious laws embodied in scriptures. The expected result is the accumulation of vast religious merit. By virtue of such religious merit, the pious hope to enjoy life on both sides of the fence of death. On this side of the fence, health, wealth, happiness, longevity, success, power, position, prestige, reputation, etc. are expected. Sometimes this expectation may not be fulfilled. But even so, the rewards awaiting the pious on the other side of the fence—supernatural delights, abundance of facilities, unrestricted fulfilment of wishes, etc.—are guaranteed by supernatural authority. No power on earth can stand in the way of the pious proceeding to enjoy supernatural rewards when he is admitted into the kingdom of heaven after death.

In the second place, spiritual action may mean selfless action performed in the best interests of society. Man advances beyond ritualism and ceremonialism when he realizes that true virtue lies in unmotivated acts of goodness. Such acts of charity as feeding the hungry, nursing the sick, etc. amount to virtue only if they are performed out of genuine love and not as a device for personal aggrandisement. Regard for social welfare and progress, not scriptural injunction, is the ultimate standard of spiritual action. True sacrifice is not a matter of rites and ceremonies. It is in essence a sincere self-offering at the altar of social good. In that sense our whole life is to become an act of sacrifice to the Idea of Good.

At the beginning the notion of selfless social action is considerably restricted by considerations of class interest and social status. A person born in a warrior family is taught that his life-mission lies in functioning as a warrior even though he may have the temperament and inner potential to become a successful businessman or creative artist. A person born in a business family is forced to receive training in business even though he may have the talent for the career of a diplomat or religious leader. Similarly, a person born in a bourgeois family is taught that his highest duty lies in selfless dedication to the safeguarding of bourgeois interest. A person born in a proletarian or peasant family is taught that his highest duty lies in selfless dedication to the best interest of the proletarian or peasant class of society. Thus ethical duty is conceived in terms of one's conventionally fixed position in society or ideologically conceived class interest. This is undoubtedly a very narrow conception of ethical duty or spiritual ideal of action. Even though it may be necessary at a certain stage of social evolution or under certain circumstances, in modern times it is a sheer anachronism. It involves a colossal waste of individual talent. It dries up the roots of culture and progress.

In the third place, spiritual action may mean selfless dedication to human welfare on the basis of one's free self-development. To be true to one's own self is the first pre-requisite of social service. That is the only way of offering one's best to society. The first and foremost duty of every individual is to develop his own latent possibilities. In doing so, an individual born in a clerical family may choose to receive training and education as a soldier or executive officer. A person born in a bourgeois family may choose to prepare himself as a champion of the social underdog. A person born in a proletarian family may choose the ideal of upholding justice with regard to conflicting social interests. A person born in a militant racial group or aggressive nation may choose the ideal of a revolutionary social reformer or international peacemaker. Freedom of choice is indeed the essential condition of the full growth of personality, and of the maximum use of human talent.

Having developed himself to the full, true to the essence of his individuality, the yogi of action proceeds to promote human welfare in a spirit of non-attachment. Non-attachment implies the sacrifice of personal profit and comfort at the altar of social good. Non-attachment also implies the transcending of one's ego in the discovery of a universal creative principle operative in life and history. A true yogi of action seeks to advance the cause of human welfare not as a self-righteous or self-important bigwig. He acts as an humble instrument of the supreme Being which is the source of all higher values.

According to much of the traditional interpretation of the yoga of action, selfless social activity is a means to the attainment of individual salvation. It brings about increasing self-perfection eventually resulting in spiritual liberation (*mukti*). The individual's union with the eternal is the goal, social and humanitarian action is the means. When the former is attained, the need for the latter is naturally outgrown. Whether such union with the eternal assumes the form of wisdom or devotion (*jñāna* or *bhakti*) is a controversial issue into which we need not enter here. According to devotees, selfless action leads to perfect devotion which is the immediate cause of liberation or rather the very essence of liberation. According to contemplatives, selfless action leads to perfect wisdom which is the immediate cause of liberation or rather the very essence of liberation.

Integral yoga maintains that selfless action is not only a means but also an essential aspect of the ultimate goal. It is certainly a means to the attainment of spiritual freedom. But it is also the most vital content of that freedom. It is the spontaneous outpouring of authentic freedom.

Spiritual freedom in its fullness is neither an abstraction nor a transcendent flight. It is not to be conceived onesidedly as detached knowledge or supernatural devotion. It is the unity of knowledge, love and fruitful action. It is the wisdom that affirms life and the world as the field of manifestation of the eternal. It is the love that is vitally concerned in the progress of civilization. It is the action that releases the creative energies of the soul. It is the full flowering of personality, in which the intellectual, emotional and volitional aspects of human nature obtain a new fulfilment and a unique transformation. Having attained authentic freedom, the individual experiences the oneness of all existence and perceives the dynamic significance of life and history. Experience of unity produces the spirit of love and compassion. Perception of the dynamic significance of life prompts him to act for the good of humanity out of the fullness of love. Such action may be called illuminated action. It is essentially free and spontaneous. It knows no law except the law of love. It knows no purpose except the cosmic purpose of existence. It is unfettered co-operation with the world-spirit in creating ever higher values in the onward march of civilization.

INTEGRAL (PŪRṆA) YOGA

Integral yoga represents a modern synthesis of the traditional yoga systems of India. It exposes their inadequacy and onesidedness, and incorporates into itself the elements of truth embedded in them. It gives yoga an affirmative and dynamic form. It places the spiritual ideal of life on the foundation of an integrated world-view such as takes into account the evolutionary and historical perspective of life.

For integral yoga the ultimate goal of life is complete self-integration. Action, love, wisdom and peace are equally important elements in such self-integration. They are inseparable aspects of man's integral union with Being. Exaggerated emphasis upon any one of these values exalted above others disturbs the balance of life. Extremist and one-sided tendencies are the root cause of conflict and suffering.

The yoga of love is perfectly right in affirming love as the fulfilment of life and as an essential ingredient of salvation. But integral yoga points out that love in its full flowering is inseparable from wisdom and selfless action. Love is not subjection to overwhelming waves of emotion such as carry a man off his feet. It is not sentimentalism such as suffocates action or makes it ineffectual. It is not emotional fixation upon any particular symbol of God or authority symbol such as a god-man, a book of revelation, a preceptor or guru, a fixed dogma or creed or ideology, etc. Such emotional fixation is damaging to the free growth of personality. Devotion to authority symbols has its value within certain limits as a source of spiritual nourishment and as an agency for self-discipline. But when such devotion smothers the flowering of individuality, it spells ruin and stagnation. In due course devotion to authority must yield place to devotion to truth and the spirit of progress. Love is not emotional fixation, but ever-expanding appreciation of the glory of the spirit. Nor is love a kind of rapturous dalliance with some supernatural Deity such as removes the mystic from the field of action and social relationship.

Love in its spiritual essence is an attribute of wisdom. It flows from the vision of the interdependence of all life and the oneness of all existence. It is active interest in the progress and betterment of society. It is the joyful expression of the soul emancipated from the bonds of selfishness. It is a function of the free spirit in man. In the pure flame of love the impurities of attachment and possessiveness are burnt to ashes. Love is undivided loyalty to life's higher values. It is active regard for the welfare of humanity as a form of manifestation of the Divine.

The yoga of knowledge is perfectly right in affirming knowledge as the fulfilment of life and an essential ingredient of salvation. But integral yoga points out that knowledge in its full flowering is inseparable from love and action. Knowledge in its spiritual essence is not merely an affair of the intellect but the self-shining of the total integrated self. It is not a kind of ivory-tower contemplation or cloistered meditation characterized by lack of concern in the weal and woe of society. It is not a rejection of the realm of nature as evil. It is not a repudiation of the phenomenal as illusory or unreal. It is not a mere ignoring of the existential status of the world with a view to the contemplation of ideas, forms and essences. Nor is knowledge to be regarded as blissful absorption in the bosom of the Absolute or Emptiness.

Knowledge in its essence is comprehensive awareness of the nature of existence. It is the vision of things as they are. It reveals the dark disquieting and destructive features of life as well as the brilliant inspiring and creative possibilities of life. It focuses attention upon the status and function of the individual in the total scheme of existence. It also awakens him to the timeless dimension of being which is the source of ultimate peace and freedom. Thus knowledge provides the link between freedom and action, between transcendent peace and social existence.

The yoga of action is perfectly right in affirming action as the essence of human reality and as an essential condition of salvation. But integral yoga points out that action is not merely a means to self-purification resulting in salvation. There is room for total action even after the attainment of salvation. In point of truth, really selfless action begins only after salvation. The liberated individual acts by way of participating in the creative adventure of life. His action assumes the form of free co-operation with the evolving world-spirit. His action is not a mere concession to the requirements of social existence. It is total and joyful self-giving at the altar of man's collective good.

Liberated action rises above the limits imposed by scriptural injunctions and fixed cultural patterns. It may assume the revolutionary form of introducing new ideas and setting new patterns. It involves a transvaluation of the values of life. Stemming from a vision of new values, it breaks the outworn norms of behaviour. Entrenched in the profound peace of the soul, it is unfettered by considerations of personal profit and loss. Armed with the authority of the eternal, it pays no heed to the favour or frown of established authority. At the same time by virtue of a firm hold upon the realities of the human situation, it accomplishes its purpose to perfection.

A dominant tendency of traditional yoga and mysticism is to visualize the spiritual destiny of man negatively as emancipation from the bonds of Nature (*prakṛti*). An unbridgeable gulf is believed to exist between nature and spirit, between body and soul. Consequently, religious striving so often assumes the form of an uncompromising struggle between the flesh and the spirit. All forms of self-torture and mortification of the flesh are invented in order to help in the triumph of the spirit. The happiness of social life is rejected as the siren song of the flesh. It is assumed that one has to go to the wilderness in order to contact the spirit.

According to integral yoga, freedom is not emancipation *from* Nature, but emancipation *in* Nature. It is not liberation *from* society, but liberation *in* society—in the midst of a thousand bonds of social relationship. It is not an escape from the fetters of the flesh, but a transformation thereof as a fit instrument of the spiritual ends of existence.

There are several reasons why many mystics have been inclined to take a negative attitude to the body. They have looked upon the body as a burden to dispose of or a prison-house to escape from. They have practised all kinds of austerity and self-mutilation as the one way of salvation.

One obvious reason is to be found in the false religious teaching that sex is a sin and that physical pleasure derived from good food, warm clothing, comfortable living, companionship of the opposite sex, etc. is a temptation of the devil. At the utmost sex is grudgingly and provisionally approved as a means of perpetuating the human race. For the purpose of procreation sex thus becomes a necessary evil. But beyond this purpose it is the devil's trap. For an all-out spiritual seeker sex is considered the gateway to hell under all circumstances. That is why he has to reject family and social life and take to asceticism. Sex as a source of pleasure is a taboo. Sex as a healthy expression of genuine love between man and woman is a double taboo. Similarly, eating is grudgingly accepted as a necessary means of maintaining the body. Eating as a source of pleasure is also a taboo.

The dualistic thinking which trenchantly separates spirit from nature is the metaphysical basis of such perverted teaching. So the metaphysically oriented ascetic proceeds to exorcise the devil from his body in the name of purification. Everytime he feels the irrepressible strength of his instinctual drives, he is assailed with terrible guilt feelings. A compulsive need for punishment prompts him to indulge in further mortification of the flesh. Moreover, his impetuous search for the spirit makes him negligent of his body in various ways. He passes sleepless nights. He forgets to relax. He boasts of his ability for prolonged fasting. As a result, lack of sufficient rest and sleep and of adequate nourishment increasingly devitalizes the body. Serious ailments are contracted. Ulcer, asthma, cancer, etc. become usual accompaniments of the ascetic's life. But bodily devitalization and disease seem to serve the ascetic's purpose pretty well. They assuage his guilt feelings and satisfy his need for punishment. They also furnish him with weapons with which to fight his deadly foe, to wit, sex. The body thus continues to be the hiding place of unfulfilled instinctual drives of which the heaven-bound soul is constantly in fear. Inner conflict and tension speeds up his ethereal flight. One-pointed ethereal flight further accentuates the inner tension. The body is thus veritably turned into a devil's dungeon or unbearable prison-house. No other solution is left except the way of self-destruction in some form or other. Belief in ethereal immortality comes handy to rationalize the will to die.

For an integral yogi the ultimate goal is neither ethereal immortality nor the realization of the spirit to the neglect of the body. He aims at the integral development of mind, body and soul. He disdains extremist tendencies and onesided efforts at self-perfection. The balanced growth of personality—complete self-integration or integral self-realization—is his ideal.

In integral yoga due recognition is given to the importance of natural instincts and impulses in the scheme of self-development. Organized and intelligent fulfilment of normal instincts is considered an essential factor in the growth of personality. Such fulfilment alone can lay the stable foundation for spiritual unfoldment.

According to integral yoga, Nature is no enemy of the spirit. On the contrary, she conceals the spirit in her bosom. As we co-operate with Nature, she affords us an ever-deepening insight into the glory of the spirit. She herself helps us to transcend her lower forms and discover her higher forms. She helps us to outgrow sensuous modes of enjoyment and discover intellectual, moral and mystical modes of self-fulfilment. Radical differences of quality, lower and higher sets of values, are inherent in the evolutionary scheme of Nature. The values designated spiritual are no less an essential part of the spirit of Nature than the values designated material. The spirit may be defined as the higher mode of fulfilment of the creativity of Nature. And Nature may be regarded as the self-expressive energy and evolutionary dynamism of the spirit.

The dualism of matter and mind, nature and spirit, is inherent in the same evolutionary flux. Spiritual values emerge naturally and dualistically out of the organized and intelligent fulfilment of material values. This is the dialectic of Nature. This may also be called the dialectic of the spirit in Nature. When man intelligently co-operates with Nature, she rewards him with the treasures of the spirit. Material Nature herself helps him to transcend materiality and realize the spiritual potentiality hidden in her depth.

A child's natural instinct is to play with toys and dolls. If he is prevented from the fulfilment of this natural desire, all his life he will nurse a secret neurotic longing for the suppressed playful instincts of childhood. It will obstruct his unfettered growth in the direction of other interests. Whereas when the child's play instinct is given due recognition and legitimate outlet, the time soon comes when he outgrows his interest in toys. His mind now turns to other interests such as the companionship of real friends of the same sex. As he goes through this phase affirmatively, his interest is further expanded to embrace friends of the opposite sex. Artificial suppression of heterosexual desires can prove devastating for health, longevity and social adjustment. A huge amount of psychic energy is tied up in the ill-conceived task of keeping them suppressed. All manner of neurotic disturbances, eccentricities, etc. may result therefrom. A sense of estrangement from the world develops. An emotionally starved person feels like a stranger in this world. He feels the psychic need to condemn the natural world and the social environment as either unreal or thoroughly evil. Consequently, he begins to move further and further away from society and civilization. His is an one-track mind, one-sided in its interest.

But duly satisfied, the sex energy undergoes miraculous transformations. Through organized and intelligent fulfilment, it gives rise to growing interest in social service, humanitarian work, and ethical dedication. A vast amount of psychic energy is released and reoriented towards such other interests as science, art, ethics and religion within the framework of a balanced outlook on life.

In the course of inner self-development an individual may one day attain a sudden cataclysmic spiritual experience. It is the intuitive awareness of the eternal in man, of the timeless dimension of existence. It seems to involve a complete break with the past. It is the experience of being reborn in an entirely new world. For a person who has been onesided in his religious search—who left unfinished the task of coming to terms with the unconscious psyche with its instinctual urges—this radical experience of spiritual intuition may provide justification for the rejection of nature and society in favour of the timless. He sees no reconciliation between the world of space-time and the supreme Being which is beyond space and time. In delivering the message of eternity, he denies the values of time.

But the integral yogi experiences the identity of the world of time and the timeless Being. Having discovered his roots in the eternal, he appreciates the significance of the world of space-time as the ever-expanding field of manifestation of the eternal. Integration of personality lays the foundation for an integrated outlook on life.

In integral self-realization, the growth of personality is as important as the vision of the superpersonal. The growth of personality involves the optimum development of the physical, emotional, intellectual and moral aspects of existence. It implies organized fulfilment of normal human desires. It requires a coming to terms with the instinctual drives of personality and a harmonization of passion and reason. At the other end, the vision of the superpersonal is the essence of mystic experience. It is the discovery of that timeless transcendence in which man is rooted.

The growth of personality brings power and love. It brings wisdom in human relations and the ability for efficient action. On the other hand, awareness of the eternal brings profound peace and full freedom. It brings ontological insight and compassion. It represents a vision of new values and the hidden possibilities of life. Integral yoga aims at the unity of personality growth and spiritual intuition. It affirms the ideal of integrated personality as a creative centre of expression of the eternal. It affirms the ideal of manifesting the Divine in the evolutionary march of society and civilization.

CHAPTER V

BASIC PRINCIPLES OF INTEGRAL YOGA

We have seen that integral yoga defines the spiritual destiny of life as dynamic and complete self-integration. It is important to realize the inmost essence of one's own being as a unique centre of creative self-expression of Being.

There are three essential ingredients in the realization of complete self-integration: psychic integration, cosmic integration, and existential integration.

PSYCHIC INTEGRATION

Psychic integration implies a harmonization of the different aspects of personality. There are some conflicting elements of human nature. Instinctual drives, impulses and urges are inherent in the unconscious psyche. In opposition to many of them is the rational will of the conscious mind. The conscious rational will is moulded by the social and cultural forces of the community to which an individual belongs.

The unconscious psyche is the source of limitless energy. It is the power house of the individual. Besides the sexual impulse it includes the vital impetus to grow and develop. It includes the holistic impulse, the drive to attain ever-widening wholeness of being, as well as the self-assertive will to power. It is the habitat of repressed wishes and desires as well as original creative urges. The unconscious is indeed the region where the vulgar and the sublime, the demon and the angel, dwell side by side. It is where light is hidden in darkness, and darkness is capable of turning into light.

The unconscious psyche carries in its deepest layer memories of the protracted evolution of the human race. Crucial experiences of evolving mankind are deposited therein as archetypal images. The symbol of God as the cosmic father or the cosmic mother is operative there as a dynamic force. Symbols of the eternal child and the eternal feminine, of the grand old man and the malicious witch, are part of the inheritance of the unconscious. Symbols of the serpent as irrational impulse and of the bird as the high-soaring intellect, do also belong to the structure of the unconscious.

Man's rational consciousness is shaped by socio-cultural forces. It acquires the ideas of good and evil, of god and devil, of heaven and hell, from the cultural environment. It learns the art of self-discipline with a view to applying its psychic energy to the fulfilment of socially approved goals. It is persuaded to suppress certain promptings of the unconscious on the strength of socially recommended standards of excellence and perfection. Thus a conflict between the conscious and the unconscious, between impulse and law, is set up in various forms in the heart of the individual. When this inner conflict and tension is more than the individual can handle, all manner of emotional disturbances appear.

Various extremist and one-sided attempts are often made to resolve the inner psychic tension. Some prefer the spontaneity of passing impulse to the restraint of reason. They decide to follow indiscriminately the promptings of inward urges. They are guided by the pleasure principle or the hedonistic concept of 'Eat, drink and be merry'. But unfortunately hedonism breaks down by its inherent paradox. It proves cruelly self-defeating. The consciously pursued pleasure is ever elusive like a will-o'-the-wisp. Our keenest pleasures are those which come unexpected or as the by-product of our selfless devotion to some objective value. Moreover, when divergent desires begin to conflict with one another, there is no way to reconcile them in accordance with the pleasure principle. The result is a life of chaotic impulses pulling in different directions, or a life of aimless drifting on the flow of vanishing pleasures.

Some again prefer perfection to pleasure. They swing to the opposite pole from hedonism. They tread the rigorous path of austerity and self-immolation. They are activated by unflinching devotion to some standard of perfection held forth by society. In doing so they ruthlessly suppress inner promptings of their own unconscious mind. They allow the super-ego to become oppressive and tyrannical. A pervasive sense of human sinfulness corrodes their soul. The soaring flames of puritanism burn up their vital fluid like scorching rays of the sun. In consequence, they are likely to develop behavioral oddities and eccentricities, if not more serious psychic disturbances. They have to pay indeed a heavy price for failure to come to terms with the unconscious.

Some again may prefer an independent quest of the spirit to socially prescribed perfection. They choose the ascetic path of exclusive devotion to pure Transcendence. They decide to advance alone towards the Alone. In doing so they do not hesitate to suppress the social and humanitarian side of life. They may even develop an uncompromising attitude of hostility to society. The follies and foibles of social life, its superficiality and conventionality, may drive them to extreme antagonism and withdrawal. But in suppressing the social side, they have also to suppress some fundamental urges of the psyche. Because, in the last analysis, psyche and society are inseparable. Their all-out search for the spirit in disregard of social demands and psychic urges, may, however, by virtue of their single-minded devotion, produce some spiritual gains. Through intensification of inward consciousness they may gain unusual aesthetic insights or mystical visions. Such spiritual gains undoubtedly bring some satisfaction to the soul. But they represent only a partial achievement. The denial of the social and instinctual aspects of life means considerable self-mutilation. In scaling the heights of the spirit, one is uprooted from the depths of the psyche. One attains brilliance at the cost of wholeness. In rising up to heaven, one loses contact with mother earth. There may be a meteoric rise to prominence, but the opportunity for balanced growth and integral self-fulfilment is lost.

Psychic integration implies the harmonious growth of personality. In the interest of balanced growth, one has to come to terms with the fundamental instinctual urges of one's nature. One has to pay attention to the distinctive bent and inclination of the individual psyche. In an attempt to reconcile impulse and reason, the unconscious id and the conscious ego, one discovers a deeper principle of unity in one's existence. It is the principle of the higher self. It does not allow the lopsided development of mind at the cost of body, or of brawn at the cost of brains. It does not encourage the one-sided growth of intellect at the cost of emotion, or of sentimentalism at the sacrifice of calm judgement. It does not permit the tyrannical growth of social consciousness at the sacrifice of psychic needs or the rebellious spirit of whimsical and arbitrary behaviour such as is subversive of the social order.

Since psyche and society are essentially inseparable, one has to take into account the demands of society even for the sake of psychic growth. One has to realize that however imperfect the norms of social morality may be, one cannot reject one's fundamental relationship to society without self-mutilation. Even when one resorts to the remotest nook of solitude one carries society with oneself because society is part of one's soul. The soul has the vital need to love others and to be loved by others. Its very essence lies in relating itself to fellow beings. So, in getting away from the sphere of social relation and action, one smothers the social ingredient of the soul. One may criticize society and try to remould it, but one cannot entirely ignore society or discard it. To renounce society permanently for its imperfections is like rejecting one's wife for her illness. Likewise, to suppress the unconscious psyche for its dark impulses is like throwing away the baby with the bath water. For, the light is hidden right in the heart of darkness.

COSMIC INTEGRATION

The foregoing discussion of the need for psychic integration leads by a sort of inner dialectic to the concept of cosmic integration. The psyche cannot be fully integrated without realization of its relationship to nature and society, i.e. to the cosmos. Psyche and cosmos are inseparable aspects of one concrete reality. The fundamental reality is neither the psyche nor the cosmos but the psyche-cosmos continuum. It is neither the isolated self nor the independent universe, but the self-in-the-universe or the universe-for-the-self. It is *ātman-brahman* (thou-that or I-that).

In point of truth there is no self-enclosed entity in the universe. Relations are vital to existence. To exist is to be related. An atom exists in so far as it is related in a field of energy. A plant lives in so far as it is related in a physical environment of air, light, water and soil. An animal lives and moves in so far as it is related in various ways to its own species and other species. A human individual grows in so far as he responds in various ways to nature, to society, and to the stirring of the eternal within himself.

In order to achieve health, happiness and wholeness in one's psychic growth, one has to maintain integral relationship to the total environment including nature and society. An individual injures himself by shutting out nature from his life. That is why the artificial modes of living in many modern societies is so detrimental to health and vitality. Fresh contacts with nature are always revitalizing. Fresh air, fresh water, sunshine, open space, silent communion with the sublime in nature—such things are essential for the blossoming of the human psyche. Exposure to the beauty and grandeur of nature is a source of profound inspiration to the soul. That is why places like the Himalayan regions, the Grand Canyon, Niagara Falls, etc. have been like the home of spiritual rebirth for thousands of sensitive souls.

Harmony with nature also implies a feeling of kinship with the animal kingdom. By mercilessly killing animals, man kills the spirit within himself. By being heartless to the mute sufferings of his world mates, he smothers the finer sensibilities of his own nature. By setting himself in violent opposition to the rest of creation, he creates division and discord within his own being. Such division and discord enfeeble and disfigure his personality. One cannot achieve psychic wholeness by inflicting wounds upon the wholeness of life. A feeling of oneness with the realm of nature, a sense of life's sacredness, a reverence for all life, is indeed vital for the holistic growth of human personality.

The psyche also blossoms in the medium of social action. The more man gives himself in the spirit of love and friendship, the more he experiences the delight of self-expansion. The more he becomes vitally concerned with the welfare of fellowbeings, the more he enlarges his own being. An active interest in others is an essential means to the bursting of the ego-shell.

An individual takes his first step beyond egocentricity when he learns to subordinate his personal pleasure and comfort to the interest of his family. Or, maybe his first lesson comes from his discovery of a real 'chum' from among his circle of acquaintance. He is ready to surrender his personal likes and dislikes for the satisfaction of his chosen friend. He may even be ready to die for his or her sake.

In the course of further development the welfare of the community to which he belongs may become a distinct motive of action. Next, the welfare of the country or nation to which he belongs may become a dominant spring of action. For the sake of his nation he is ready to sacrifice his personal and family interests. He is even willing to sacrifice his life.

In the course of still further development an individual may become actively concerned with the welfare of the international human family. From 'My country, right or wrong' he now advances to the motto: 'Humanity before my country.' He feels convinced that human welfare is indivisible. The best interest of one's country is indissolubly bound up with the welfare of the world community. Or, the conviction perhaps grows in him that the ultimate good of his country is entwined with the concept of truth and justice, with the notion of God. Taking a long-range view, the policy of aggressive nationalism or militant expansionism is bound to react adversely upon the ultimate good of one's own nation. The different peoples of the world do indeed exist by being closely related to one another. They are essentially interdependent. They are inseparably associated members of the cosmic whole. They live, move and have their being in one indivisible cosmic medium. An active realization of this truth produces cosmic integration.

EXISTENTIAL INTEGRATION

But neither psychic integration nor cosmic integration can attain the fullness of actuality without the discovery of the eternal spirit, of which both psyche and cosmos are different modes of manifestation.

However much a person may be rationally convinced of the need for psychic harmony, the discord between different elements of personality such as passion and reason, instinct and intellect, emotion and understanding, etc. threaten to be irreconcilable. One may achieve a measure of compromise, but the final resolution of psychic conflicts may appear impossible on the psychic level. The secret of complete psychic harmony lies in the realization of the eternal in man—of the timeless dimension of existence. It is there that the ultimate unity of the psyche is to be found. That is why the full integration of the psyche can be accomplished only in the light of existential experience, i.e. a direct insight into the ultimate ground of existence which is timeless. An existential contact with the non-temporal abyss of Being is indeed essential for the consummation of psychic integration.

The same is also true of cosmic integration. However much one may be rationally convinced of the need for social and cosmic harmony, there seems to be a fundamental and irreconcilable discrepancy between self and society, between psyche and cosmos. It appears impossible to dissolve such discrepancy by the persuasiveness of reason. One can at best hope to achieve a certain measure of compromise between individual growth and collective good. But the secret of complete cosmic harmony lies in the realization of the timeless root of the cosmic flow—of the eternal dynamically present in evolution and history. The ultimate unity of psyche and cosmos lies hidden in the timeless depth of Being. It is only an existential plunge into the abyss of Being that can reveal the principle of social harmony. It is in the light of supra-cosmic realization that the integration of psyche and cosmos can be carried to perfection.

Thus we see that the final step in integral self-development is existential integration, i.e. integration with the ultimate ground of existence, which is timeless. The discords of time can be turned into elements of harmony only in the context of the eternal. The processes of self-adjustment to the psyche and the cosmos can be consummated only through contact with the eternal.

But we should hasten to observe here that even the eternal is not to be equated with the fullness of Being. The eternal is no doubt the most fundamental dimension of existence. But it cannot certainly be said to be the only dimension of existence. Being in its fullness is multi-dimensional. The eternal represents the element of pure transcendence in Being. It represents the mystic's unfathomable mystery, the yogi's imperturbable peace and self-poise. But Being is also manifested in time in the form of evolution and history. It has the aspect of growth, development, creative self-expression, which is inseparable from life. The historical is no less essential to the structure of reality than the non-temporal.

Mysticism is right in emphasizing the value of the eternal. But mysticism makes an error in equating the eternal with the whole of Being. Such a false equation has dominated much of traditional religious thinking. It has given rise to religious pessimism, negativism, and other-worldliness. The mystic's false equation is the opposite of secularism's error in equating time with the whole of Being. The latter has given rise to epicureanism, materialism, and nihilism. The truth is that Being is the unity of time and eternity, of evolution and transcendence. It is the unity of nature and spirit, and of the historical and the nontemporal. An integral understanding of the multi-dimensional Being is essential for the balanced growth of personality. In order to attain the wholeness of being, an individual has to be true to the kindred points of heaven and home, of eternity and time.

PRINCIPLES OF CREATIVE EXISTENCE

Now, how to achieve existential integration? And how to organize one's life in such a way that existential experience may function as the basis of harmonious and fruitful living? In other words, what are the fundamental principles of creative existence?

There are four fundamental principles of creative existence: aspiration, action, meditation and love.

The spiritual unfoldment of man involves a twofold choice or commitment. It begins with a definite decision to discover the ultimate ground of existence, i.e. to realize God. It ends with a final decision to make a supreme sacrifice of oneself for the sake of the Divine dynamically present in the world, i.e. for the sake of cosmic welfare. Aspiration is the initial decision involved in spiritual life. It is an all-out search for the eternal. It is a sincere and determined resolve to organize one's whole life on the basis of spiritual values. It is the indomitable will to find out the meaning of God in the context of one's own personal experience. Theistic arguments on the one hand and agnostic reasoning on the other are alike meaningless in the absence of concrete personal existential experience. If any actual person in history did ever have a direct glimpse of the Divine, others also must be capable of having the same in some measure. When an individual feels ready to undertake the task of gaining such a direct insight, whatever the cost involved, he has the authentic aspiration. The extent of his willingness to stake his whole life on it is the measure of his aspiration.

There is an important distinction between aspiration and ambition. Ambition is the longing of man's immediate desire-nature. It is his hankering after wealth and affluence, power and position, name and fame. But authentic aspiration is the stirring of the spirit, the divine spark, in man. While ambition is a movement of the ego, aspiration is a reaching out of the soul beyond the boundaries of the ego. It is the awakening of the super-personal factor in human personality. It is the response of man's inner being to the call of the eternal or to the impact of the evolutionary world-process. Aspiration is a calm and steady flame, in which egocentric cravings and desires are more and more consumed. Ambition is the self-assertion of the individual as an individual. Aspiration is the self-affirmation of the individual as an active centre of the universal. Aspiration evolves out of ambition at a crucial moment of inward growth. It is the transmutation of ambition by the power of self-transcendence inherent in man.

We have already observed that aspiration represents one's decision to realize the eternal and to live for the eternal. Strictly speaking, such a decision is not made, it evolves. It happens to the individual in the course of his inner growth of consciousness. It takes place in the depth of the soul, in the luminous dark of the unconscious psyche, before it appears in the mind as a conscious decision. When it emerges as the central purpose of life, a vast amount of psychic energy is released. The individual can now function with the combined resources of his personality.

Authentic aspiration is known in religion as the unqualified love of God. When the flame of such love is kindled in the soul, the whole being is set on fire. It produces an expansion of consciousness to the dimensions of the universe. Selfless action is the spontaneous outcome of such self-expansion.

So, we come now to the notion of action as the second fundamental principle of creative existence and integral growth. As we have already seen, action is of the essence of human reality. It is not only a means of attaining freedom, but also the essential content of that freedom. It is the spontaneous outpouring of that freedom.

There is no such thing as absolute inaction. Even when a man is sitting very idly, his mind becomes busy riding high on the crest of his thought-waves. He is perhaps vigorously day-dreaming. When he goes to sleep, his conscious mind is put to rest, but his unconscious psyche gets busy projecting and fulfilling in subtle form some of its buried impulses and desires. When he rejects the world of action and goes to the hills, he carries the world with him in his mind and expresses his negative reaction to the world in various ways in the medium of contemplation. Through contemplation he acts upon the world from the realm of phantasy and ideas. He also acts to suppress those of his psychic impulses and emotions which are positively oriented to the world of action. And, of course, physiological processes inside the organism are all the time going on without interruption, whether he is awake or asleep, active or idle, in society or out of society.

The most important question then about action is: How to make our action more and more meaningful? How to relate action to the cosmic purpose of existence, to the ultimate goal of evolution? How to bring action into harmony with the full freedom of the spirit?

There are certain forms of action which hinder spiritual unfoldment. They inflict damage upon the free growth of personality. They alienate man from his spiritual roots and occasion his gradual self-dissipation. They may deaden the soul and crush the spirit in man.

For instance, when action is reduced to a dull monotony, to a humdrum routine affair, it becomes an imprisonment for the human soul. Society has a responsibility to see to it that the sphere of social action does not degenerate into a dehumanizing prison-house. The same thing happens when action becomes too mechanized. When there is no room for free choice of initiative, action becomes like a dead burden for the soul. It is the spiritual duty for those who enjoy freedom, power and enlightenment, to re-fashion the social structure in such a way that action assumes the form of meaningful and joyful self-expression.

As an essential ingredient of integral yoga, the principle of action has three aspects: *self-expression*, *self-poise* and *self-donation*.

The primary task of every individual is to concentrate on the development of his latent possibilities. His course of training and education must be determined accordingly. If the inner psyche of an individual points in the direction of his future as an engineer or doctor, it is outrageous to compel him for any reason to become a businessman or a priest. If his inner psyche holds forth the image of a poet or painter, it is foolish to induce him to become a politician or tycoon. When an individual is allowed to grow according to his own unique law of becoming (*swadharma*), he can rise to the height of his possibility, and his action becomes meaningful and joyful.

This does not mean that a successful engineer must invest all his time and energy in the field of engineering. Or that, an ideal politician must devote all his time and energy to political action. Oftener than not, there are many other interests and urges in a person besides his central ideal. For instance, a politician may have a great deal of interest in gardening, in music, in writing poetry, in playing golf, etc. In that case it is a challenge to him to find time to fulfil some of these interests also consistently with his major work and responsibility as a politician. Suppression of strong psychic urges is definitely harmful to the growth of personality. A basic principle of integral yoga lies in lending an attentive ear to the inner promptings of one's own psyche. A person who discovers the inner light of his own psyche and counts it as a major factor in the decision of affairs, finds action immensely fruitful and gratifying.

Another principle of action is self-poise. A person may feel sure about the actions he should perform. He may also have a measure of control over his own actions. But he can never tell beforehand how far he will succeed in his endeavour. He does not quite know how others will react to him, or whether society will appreciate him. He may find that those very people whose welfare he intends to promote misunderstand him and even deny him. He may find out that there is no necessary connection between honest and meritorious work on the one hand and social recognition and reward on the other. So an attitude of non-attachment to consequences is very much needed to sustain him in his works of social service. When in a given situation he decides after mature deliberation that a particular course of action is good for all concerned, he may proceed to do it regardless of consequences.

In an attempt to translate one's crucial decisions into action one has to go ahead fearlessly, setting aside considerations of profit and loss, praise and blame. Such disregard of, or non-attachment to, consequences produces serene self-poise. It enables one to maintain inward calmness and even temper in the midst of all changes of fortune. One acts, and yet does not act. There is a core of imperturbable immobility to all movement. It is non-action in action. One plays one's part to the best of one's ability and leaves all consequences in the hands of Providence. One has no control over consequences anyway. Virtue has its gaze fixed upon cosmic welfare. Its ear is attuned to the call of destiny. It is sheer expediency to allow the consideration of immediate consequences an upper hand. Expediency seeks reward in outward circumstances. But virtue is its own reward. It is the joy of creative self-expression. It is the joy of self-giving to the universal.

That brings us to the third principle of action, namely, the principle of self-donation. From the spiritual point of view, the ultimate motive of action is the spirit of self-donation to cosmic welfare. It is one's dedication to the inward vision of the meaning of life and evolution. It is one's active concern with new values emerging in one's consciousness. It enables a person to stand entirely on his own. Opposition and antagonism cannot coerce him into submission. Allurement or blandishments cannot cajole him into standard conformity. His ultimate loyalty is to his inward vision of the truth. He stands alone, armed with the invincible strength of his relationship to the eternal. But precisely by virtue of his taking this stand all alone, he is offering himself without any condition or reserve at the altar of the ultimate good of humanity. His self-donation may not be in conformity with the established authority and tradition. As a consequence, it is not also conditional upon social recognition and reward. He gives himself by an act of supreme sacrifice to the unborn future of man. Unforeseeable new values emerge out of such unconditional self-giving.

MEDITATION

The courage to act alone regardless of consequences is born of the awareness of one's relationship to the eternal—of one's absolute relationship to the absolute. Meditation is the channel through which one discovers this relationship.

In the practice of integral yoga, meditation and action are inseparable. Meditation, which is the art of intensifying inward consciousness, has various methods. Some of these methods will be discussed in detail in the last two chapters of this book. Here the fundamental principles of meditation as an element of the integral approach may be briefly indicated.

There are five basic principles of integral meditation: *dynamic self-offering, psychic exploration, self-energizing, critical evaluation,* and *existential experience.*

In the practice of integral yoga, dynamic self-offering to the cosmic reality is of paramount importance. It provides the right starting point and sets the proper mental framework. The spirit of self-offering is the real beginning of integral meditation, whereas the perfection of self-offering is its ultimate goal. Of course, an individual may start with any other method of prayer or meditation particularly suited to his religious or cultural background. But if he is interested in integral self-development, he has to come round sooner or later to the concept of self-offering.

The attitude of dynamic self-offering to the cosmic reality adequately reflects the concrete human situation. The human individual is not an isolated, abstract, self-subsistent entity. He does not exist apart from the cosmic whole. He is nothing apart from his environment, natural and social. His individuality becomes meaningful only in the context of the evolutionary advance of the dynamic world-spirit. So, the method of introspection or detached self-observation, carried to the end, may prove misleading. It may easily produce extreme introversion. It often encourages the introverted to wish for static and isolated self-abiding (*kaivalya*), which may be peaceful but not productive. Isolated self-abiding is liberation negatively conceived as emancipation from the evolutionary movement of life. It is the static spiritual ideal. Enamoured of the timeless dimension of the self, it fails to appreciate the significance of the historicity of the self. Man is essentially an historical being. He cannot completely fulfil himself without actively relating himself to the march of history. Withdrawal from the historical order is a form of self-mutilation. Moreover, the static ideal is rooted in a flase conception of the self as immobile and isolated consciousness. In actual reality, the self is nothing apart from its relationship to the cosmic whole. And as a unit or member of the cosmic whole, the self is not immobile but tremendously dynamic.

The method of passive self-offering to the divine or the eternal may also prove misleading. When a person is absolutely passive in his submission to the divine, he may frequently be carried off his feet by waves of emotion or dark suggestion welling up from the depths of the unconscious. When there is total passivity or vacuum, one can never be sure how that vacuum is going to be filled. Undivine forces often masquerade in the name of God. The need for a sharp discrimination between the divine and the undivine—between what is conducive to, and what is subversive of, cosmic welfare—can never be dispensed with. Consequently, self-offering to the Divine must be accompanied by constant vigilance and discrimination so that the forces of ignorance may not allure and mislead.

The attitude of passive self-offering to the divine has often stimulated the image of blissful self-absorption in the absolute. Many mystics in the past were lured by this image. They rightly rejected the theory of the self as isolated and self-subsistent consciousness. But they could not entirely shake off the influence of the static spiritual ideal. They retained the notion of the self as immobile and detached consciousness. Only, in their view, the individual is nothing apart from the absolute. So, it is through the annihilation of individuality in the absolute that consciousness is to be realized in its passive purity.

The ideal of blissful self-absorption in the absolute is based upon the inadequate conception of the individual self as a product of ignorance (*avidyā*). According to integral philosophy, the individual self is emphatically not a product of ignorance. It is not an illusory appearance of the absolute. Nor is it a passive medium of the universal. The self is essentially a free creative centre of the universal. It is therefore through dynamic self-offering to the cosmic reality that the self can hope to realize fully its inmost essence. It is through active participation in the historical order that the self can function as a significant member of the cosmic whole.

The basic reality of life cannot be defined in terms of the universal alone. Nor can it be defined in terms of the individual self alone. It can be expressed only in some such terms as the self-as-related-to-the-universal. Self-cosmos is the indivisible unit of existence. Hence integral meditation can truly begin only with the focusing of attention upon the dynamic relationship in which the self stands related to the cosmic reality.

In practising meditation one relaxes, lets go one's mind and body, and calmly reflects upon one's ontological status as an active centre of the Divine. One offers oneself, heart and soul, to the cosmic creative principle, to the universal life force, so that one's ultimate purpose of life may be revealed. Meditation is an act of dedication to the cosmic purpose of existence. During the course of meditation, whatever thoughts, impulses, desires, feelings, memories, etc. may arise in the mind, one has to observe them with patient analysis and sympathetic understanding and offer them to the Divine, so that they can all be coherently organized around the central purpose of life.

The next important phase of meditation is self-exploration. As one gets into the mood of relaxed self-observation and self-offering to the Divine, the unconscious mind is more and more activated. One begins to probe into the depths of one's personality. Different levels of the unconscious are revealed. Repressed wishes and long-forgotten memories suddenly come to the front. Unsuspected potentialities are brought to attention. Hidden powers of the mind disclose themselves. And thus self-exploration brings about a process of self-energizing.

Self-energizing reaches its height when the divine spark in man leaps into a flame. Science tells us that a vast amount of energy is hidden in the positive nucleus of the atom and that it can be released. Similarly, there is a vast reservoir of energy hidden in the depths of the unconscious psyche. Some have called it the power of God slumbering in man. Some have called it 'the coiled power' (*kuṇḍalinī*)—the central psycho-physical power lying dormant in human personality. In the course of psychic exploration this central energy-potential is eventually activated. That marks a turning-point in one's self-development. It touches off a kind of psychic explosion, a conversion of consciousness, an undreamt-of intensification of existence. A free flow of limitless energy is set in motion. The process of meditation now becomes effortless and spontaneous. Life recaptures its original freshness. One feels the presence of a much deeper power within oneself. It appears irrepressible and all-engulfing. The supreme spiritual task now lies in channelling this boundless energy along right lines.

In dealing with power there is always a great need for careful evaluation and intelligent control. A man driving an automobile at high speed must make sure that his brakes are in good order and that he is capable of applying them at the right time. People who are in charge of atomic energy know what a tremendous responsibility it is. Various precautionary measures have to be adopted to prevent its falling into irresponsible hands or slipping into monstrous abuse. Likewise, the awakening of the fundamental energy-potential in man is a psychic breakthrough which has its brilliant promise and also its dismal danger. Unless used judiciously with proper control it may burn itself up too rapidly. Even though it may shine for a while with uncommon brightness, the dazzling glare may be short-lived. One cannot afford to trifle with high-voltage power. Even the spiritual longing has to be duly restrained. The presence of power calls for patience and calm judgement. A mature sense of responsibility is needed. A clear sense of values must provide direction to the vital impulse.

Meditation is not an exercise in occultism. Without an insight into the higher values of life, occult power may prove destructive to self and society alike. That is why critical evaluaticn is an essential ingredient of meditation. The more a person is sincere in his self-offering to the cosmic reality, the more his sense of values is sharpened. The more a person is purified in heart with his flaming dedication to the supreme, the more he is lifted above the corrupting influence of powers. But after the ground has been prepared with purity of the heart and clarity of the vision of truth, power assumes the form of divine grace. It enables one to make giant strides towards the fulfilment of one's destiny.

The final phase of meditation is existential experience. It means some kind of direct insight into the ultimate ground of existence. In Buddhism this insight has been called *bodhi* or *prajñā*. Zen calls it *satori*. In Hindu philosophy it is called *samādhi* or *jñāna*. It involves a sense of rootedness in the eternal and a feeling of oneness with the universal. There is an immediate experience of the oneness of all existence. All the multitudinous forms of being, the innumerable living creatures, the divergent peoples, races and nations of the world, are experienced as unified in this ultimate ground. The apprehension of the ultimate has been called unitive or cosmic consciousness by Christian mystics. All the great religions of the world, specially the foremost mystics in world religions, point to the unitive cosmic consciousness as the crowning fulfilment of man's spiritual effort.

From the psychological point of view, existential experience signifies the awareness of a hitherto obscure and veiled new dimension of existence—the dimension of the non-temporal. The non-temporal is the abode of transcendence and freedom. When a person makes an existential contact with the non-temporal, he has an exciting sense of liberation from all bonds. In respect of his non-temporal mode of existence he rises above the sphere of cause and effect. He breaks the fetters of the law of karma. He enters upon a new phase of life—the life of participation in the timeless consciousness. The freedom and spontaneity which were lost in outgrowing childhood are now recaptured on a higher plane.

The child's spontaneity is based upon untutored impulse and unknowing innocence. It is an unstable equilibrium. The development of reason and conscience is sure to disturb it. As the child is introduced to the socio-cultural dualities of good and evil, god and devil, heaven and hell, etc. his freshness and spontaneity are gone. He experiences some kind of fall from paradise. Along with strife and struggle, a life of taboos and inhibitions begins. But the holistic growth of personality may eventually result in discovery of the non-temporal dimension of being. Upon such discovery freedom and spontaneity reappear on a stable basis. Paradise is regained on a deeper level of personality. Neither the temptation of devil nor the wrath of God can destroy it any more. The conflicting noises of life's power politics are hushed into silence in the sanctuary of the timeless.

LOVE OR LĪLĀ

Broadly speaking, there are two levels of awareness of the non-temporal. First, the non-temporal is experienced as abstract transcendence. The pulse and the heart-beat of the world process are not felt there. The music of the spheres has no responsibe chord there. The ebb and flow of the tide of cosmic evolution is not registered there. Naturally therefore on this level of ontological insight one says 'No' to the world. The drama of life fades into unreality. The discords of evolution dissolve like a bad dream. The mystic denial reaches its highest point.

But on a deeper level of awareness of the non-temporal, the mystic denial itself is denied in a higher affirmation. The non-temporal is now perceived to enfold within itself the profoundest secret of the world process. The evolutionary movement of life and history reappears clothed in a new significance. It is realized that if the world is nothing apart from God, God is nothing apart from the world. God is the unity of the world. The world is the diversified expression of God. The dichotomy of God and world is dissolved in the non-duality of the non-temporal. The perspective of the non-dual non-temporal lends a profound meaning to the dynamic presence of God-in-the-world.

The affirmative awareness of the non-temporal may be termed integral existential experience. It is the apprehension of the ground of existence as the indefinable unity of God and the world. Such integral experience is the basis of illumined creative living. It is the basis of love as selfless participation in the creative advance of cosmic evolution. In Hindu philosophy such participation has been called *līlā*, i.e. joyful co-operation with the dynamic world-spirit (*Kṛṣṇa*). This is the significance of Śrī Kṛṣṇa's exhortation to Arjuna in the Bhagavadgītā. Kṛṣṇa advises Arjuna to be inwardly united with the Divine and outwardly act on the battlefield of life. He is to act in a spirit of fellowship with the Divine. The objective of such action is to carry to fruition the purpose of human evolution. It is to establish the kingdom of truth, justice and progress. But since it is the purpose of evolution itself, the best way to serve it is to abandon one's selfish motives and personal attachments. Purest action is that which is free from any tension of inner conflict or any compulsion of emotional attachment.

Līlā is cosmic love. It is the crowning glory of integral yoga. It is not static union with the eternal. It is not the peace of self-annihilation in the absolute. It is not the ecstasy of life and world negation. Nor is it a mode of ego-fulfilment. The pure flame of cosmic love leaps into being only through the burning of the ego. There are some who shy away from immediate contact with the eternal in order to preserve their personal wishes and predilections, their attachments and emotional bonds. They are eager to participate in life with their egocentric individuality kept intact. They are unwilling to relinquish their inherited and ingrained notions of good and evil, god and devil. This may be called ethical love. It shows active interest in social amelioration. But it is afraid of rising above social morality in favour of a direct encounter with the eternal. The naked touch of the eternal is devastating to the fixed notions of conventional morality and dogmatic theology. It effectuates a radical transvaluation of values. It crucifies egocentric individuality with all its pet desires and flattering creeds.

For integral yoga cosmic love is the secret of self-perfection. It is dynamic love of the Divine actively engaged in the world process. It is non-attached love of the world as visible manifestation of the Divine. It is participation in the being of the world with a self-poise in the heart of non-being. A person who contacts the eternal has no more any sense of external compulsion or socially imposed obligation. When he acts for the good of humanity, he acts with a sense of full freedom and with the joy of spontaneity. Having had a glimpse of the ultimate meaning of life, he cannot turn away into the peace of private seclusion and stoic indifference. He feels the luminous urge within himself to fulfil his role in the cosmic drama to the best of his ability and in a spirit of supreme dedication to cosmic welfare.

CHAPTER VI

THE PHILOSOPHY OF INTEGRAL YOGA

INTEGRAL yoga is based upon a comprehensive philosophical outlook. It is the outlook of integral non-dualism. The essentials of integral non-dualism may be presented here in a brief outline.

Philosophy has always been concerned with a search for some ultimate unifying principle of the universe. It has tried to discover some principle of unity in terms of which the manifoldness of the world can be embraced in a synoptic vision.

The ancient Greek philosopher Thales found the ultimate philosophical principle in water and attempted to derive the world out of water. 'If you take away all water,' he said, 'the world will be reduced to a heap of ashes. Add water and it will blossom like a rose.' But Anaximander replaced water by air, a subtler element, as the supreme philosophic principle. Then Heraclitus put forward fire as the ultimate principle. Conflicting claims and counter-claims thus began to rend the philosophic air. Conflict sharpened criticism, and criticism resulted in growing scepticism. But in course of time it was realized that water, air, fire, etc. can at best be regarded as mere symbols of the absolute. None of them as determinate forms of existence can be equated with the absolute. The absolute must essentially be formless in order to embrace and creatively sustain the endless forms of being. It must essentially be indeterminable in order to unify countless determinations. Mysticism at its best in all countries has tried to communicate this precious truth.

Philosophers influenced by natural science or physics have advanced the notion of matter or energy as the basic principle of unity in terms of which the world can be explained. This has given rise to materialism which has assumed various forms in history. Philosophers influenced by biology have advanced the concept of universal life force, the *élan vital*, as the philosophic principle. They have endeavoured to derive matter, mind, spirit, etc. from the free creativity of the vital impetus. This has given rise to vitalism with its various forms in history. Philosophers influenced by psychology and personal psychic experience have adduced the concept of mind, psyche, or some specific psychic function, as the fundamental principle of explanation. Thus the notions of universal mind, unconscious will, the will to power, the collective unconscious, etc. have gained ontological significance. Subjective idealism in some form or other has been the outcome.

Philosophers who have been dominated in their thinking by the categories of religious experience have regarded Spirit or God as the ultimate principle. Religious monotheism affirms the reality of one God as the supreme ruler of the universe. He is the creative source of both matter and mind, nature and man. He is endowed with such attributes as wisdom, righteousness, mercifulness, love, redemption, omnipresence, omnipotence, etc. But in so far as God is placed beyond the natural world up there somewhere in the high heavens, in spite of all his omnipotence He can hardly be regarded as the ultimate philosophical principle of unity. The true absolute must embrace within itself the distinctions of nature and spirit, world and God. The external existence of the world makes the God of monotheism relative to the world as much as the world is relative to God. Consistently developed religious philosophy must eventually overcome the dualism of God and the world. It has to affirm God as the absolute spirit which embraces and pervades the world and at the same time transcends it in respect of its immeasurable richness of content. A personal and determinate Absolute is a contradiction in terms. God conceived in terms of determinate qualities and powers is at best an exalted symbol of the absolute. He cannot be equated with the absolute. He is the absolute as it appears to the human mind.

Philosophers who have been dominated by the categories of ethics have equated the absolute with the ethical will to progress, the striving for continuous development and perfection. For them the world is a ceaseless process of evolution advancing to higher and higher levels of moral perfection. It is perpetual becoming, progressive self-perfection.

But moralistic philosophy or ethical idealism pretty soon finds itself in a dilemma. Is the cosmic will to progress intrinsically perfect or imperfect? If perfect, the striving for perfection becomes meaningless. If imperfect, it ceases to be the absolute. It must be aware of an external standard of perfection to which it wishes to conform. It finds itself wanting in the balance of that external standard. What is that superior reality which furnishes the standard of perfection?

Viewing the matter from another standpoint, the question may be raised: Is the ethical ideal of perfection an attainable or unattainable goal? In the former case, as soon as the ideal is attained, life must go out of business. There would be no other incentive left to the process of becoming. Evolution would come to a dead end. If on the contrary the ideal of perfection be regarded as unattainable, the notion of progress becomes meaningless. There can be no advance towards an ever-receding horizon. A thousand steps towards an unattainable goal are no better than ten steps forward, because both these efforts equally fall short of the ideal. Measured against the infinite, all finite beings are equally finite and imperfect. The truth is that the concept of evolution as an asymptotic approximation to an ever-receding goal is self-contradictory. It also contradicts the profoundest spiritual experiences of man. A thoroughly integrated person seems somehow to go beyond all striving and straining and to touch the bedrock of timeless Being. The conflict and tension of becoming are replaced within him by the profound peace of being. The anguish of ethical struggle is overcome with the joy and love of union with the infinite. A saint becomes a sage through the discovery of Being as the transcendent source of all ethical distinctions.

It may further be noted that an unbiased study of the actual process of evolution and history gives a direct lie to the moralistic interpretation of the universe. Man's moral notions are too narrow a measuring rod to fathom the mystery of the world process. They are too relative and parochial to be used as a key even to the history of civilization. Such amoral forces as the will to live and survive, the lust for power, personal vanity, chauvinistic nationalism, aggressive collectivism, etc. seem to be the most potent determinants of history. If there is any cosmic determinant ultimately overriding such individual and collective motivations, it is too much of an unfathomable mystery to be expressed in terms of human morality. The cosmic force of evolution is essentially amoral or supra-moral.

If the absolute be amoral, it is also alogical. Reality divided by logic always leaves a remainder. The multiform fullness of reality always slips through the meshes of logical notions. But still the philosophers whose main approach has been logical and dialectical have often equated the absolute with Idea or Reason. Idea as the logical universal has been affirmed as the ultimate unifying principle of the universe. For Plato the highest idea is the Idea of Good which embraces in a teleological structure all other ideas or universals. It includes on the one hand such value concepts as truth, beauty, freedom, etc. and such class essences as plantness, animality, humanity, etc. But the notion of formless matter becomes an uncomfortable enigma. As a fundamental ingredient of our world of experience it must be accepted as a metaphysical principle. But as devoid of all form and essence—as the negation of idea—it must be rejected as non-being. The world of our experience is still more of a riddle. It is a hybrid product torn between being and non-being, between form and matter. It is a realm of shadows and imitations.

For Hegel the absolute is the Idea conceived as the comprehensive and self-coherent organism of such fundamental categories as being, non-being, becoming, matter, mind, individual, universal, etc. The Idea externalizes itself in Nature and increasingly fulfils itself in history. The products of human culture such as society, art, religion, philosophy, state, etc. are various modes of increasing self-fulfilment of the Idea. But an unbiased and open-minded observation of nature and history discloses the presence of the irrational and the absurd in the world process. Nature is the abode of the immediate, the absolutely given element, which can by no means be resolved into a rational scheme of relations, a complex of ideas and essences. History is the home of the alogical. It is a chronicle of volcanic eruptions from the non-rational depths of the human psyche. It is a record of changes in society occasioned by forces much deeper than reason, calculation, and logical speculation.

The fact that there are alogical and amoral aspects of reality does not entail that logic and morality are void of ontological significance. There are without doubt features of existence which are amenable to logical understanding and moral evaluation. The vital role of mathematics in scientific progress demonstrates the fact that reality has a logical and relational structure. The vital role of ethics in the improvement of human relations and collective living demonstrates the fact that reality is the ultimate locus of all values. Reality being a dynamic and creative flow, with the change of times and circumstances the necessity always arises for a reformulation of values. Now, those philosophers who are exclusively influenced by mystic experience such as *bodhi*, *satori*, *samādhi*, unitive consciousness, vision of the heavenly Father, etc. have a tendency to minimize the logical and ethical aspects of reality and to over-emphasize the non-rational and the supra-moral. They identify the absolute as the mystical or the mysterious non-temporal.

Various attempts have been made to convey the essence of the non-temporal. It has been described as indeterminable being (*nirguṇa*), as suchness or thatness (*tathatā*). It has been described as the void or emptiness (*śūnyatā*). It is the pure nudity of Being or unfathomable Nothingness. It is the quiet incommunicable Silence (*Śānta*). It is the 'peace that passeth the understanding'. It is the nameless One or the formless Identity. It is 'the deep dazzling darkness' impenetrable to all human concepts. It is the non-rational Numinous, 'the mysterious tremendum', which outsoars all logical notions. It is that pure transcendence in which all distinctions and relations are submerged. It is that non-verbal plenum which baffles all the resources of human language.

Now the apprehension of indeterminable being which is identical with non-being can easily lead to an over-emphasis upon the non-temporal. An over-emphasis upon the non-temporal can easily lead to its equation with the absolute. Such an equation (the eternal = the absolute) produces a counter-error to that of exclusive preoccupation with the values of time. It sets up mysticism as a counter-error to that of secularism. It would easily engender an attitude of world and life negation. If the non-temporal be the ultimate reality, the world process in time must be unreal in the ultimate reference. The historical order is emptied of ultimate value and significance. Life appears to be at best a preparation for blissful union with the eternal. At its worst it is a nightmare, a dreadful prison-house for the human soul or a vicious circle of painful life, death and rebirth.

But a philosophical outlook which fails to appreciate the reality of life and the significance of history stands self-condemned. So its underlying major premise that the non-temporal equals the absolute must be wrong. The non-temporal is without doubt the most fundamental aspect of reality. It is the ultimate ground of existence. But nonetheless it is only an aspect or dimension, not the totality, of the multiform fullness of Being. It is no doubt the foundation of existence. But existence has also its superstructure of ever-emergent values in the historical medium. The absolute can therefore be no less than the unity of the non-temporal and the historical. It is Being in its multi-dimensional fullness.

The question may be raised here, How about the pluralistic philosophers who do not believe in any ultimate unifying principle of the universe? How about thinkers like William James and Bertrand Russell who talk about a pluralistic universe or logical atomism? It seems that they are right in rejecting unity as a unitary metaphysical substance. An all-embracing metaphysical substance designated God or Absolute is an unverifiable hypothesis or an intellectual construction. It commits the mistake of exalting the category of the one to the rank of the absolute. But in combating the monistic fallacy, pluralistic philosophers seem to make the counter-mistake of exalting the category of the many to the rank of the absolute. They invest pluralism with absolute and ultimate significance. They tacitly assume that the many have ontological priority over the one. The truth of the matter is that one and many are just our human categories, our human ways of arranging and comprehending the datum of experience. Being has certainly an aspect which lends itself to pluralistic interpretation. But Being has also an aspect—the aspect of non-relational continuum—which lends itself to monistic interpretation. In ultimate analysis, however, the concrete fullness of existence transcends both pluralistic and monistic interpretations. The fullness of being is non-dual, non-verbal, non-conceptual. It is in essence beyond number, quantity, quality and concept. Being is not to be equated with any symbolical structure or categorical scheme, whether monistic or pluralistic.

Broadly speaking, there are three essential aspects of reality: the pure non-temporal, the dynamic universal, and the unique individual. They are closely interrelated, interpenetrative and inseparable aspects of the same indivisible Being.

THE NON-TEMPORAL DIMENSION OF BEING (ŚIVA)

It has already been noted that the non-temporal dimension of existence outsoars all categories of the human mind. It is pure transcendence. It is existence as absolute freedom. It has been the ultimate source of inspiration to great artists, mystics, and sages the world over. It is the ultimate goal of man's spiritual effort. The evolutionary movement of life has its deep roots here.

The non-temporal is not to be regarded as the unchanging permanent substance of the world. Substance and quality are categories of the human mind. They are our subjective modes of apprehension of the real. They represent a certain manner of interpreting experience, influenced by the linguistic structure of some ethnic groups. Likewise, change and permanence are also polarized notions of the human mind. The non-temporal is not a substance that abides in change, nor a thing that defies change. It is, strictly speaking, no-thing, no-substance, no-object. It is that supreme light which reveals all things, objects, substances. It is the pure indefinable being (*tat sat*) which is identical with non-being (*śūnyatā*).

The non-temporal is that ultimate ground of existence in which subject and object, mind and matter, are unified. So it is a mistake to describe the non-temporal as the cosmic mind, universal matter, cosmic soul, etc. The latter represent divergent components of the cosmic whole. The non-temporal is the sustaining dimension of the cosmic whole. It is not to be equated with matter, mind, soul, spirit, etc. either severally or collectively.

An insight into the non-temporal has a profoundly liberating influence in life. It implies a universal perspective, a comprehensive vision of the truth. It reveals, for instance, the essential unity of all religions. Different theological conceptions of God disclose themselves as different ways of expressing the eternal mystery of life. Different world religions endeavour to guide people in different ways towards a glimpse of the non-temporal. In the absence of any sense of the non-temporal, people become dogmatic and even fanatical. They turn a dogma into absolute truth, a creed into the last word of wisdom. In claiming finality for a relatively valid idea, they turn validity into falsehood. In the name of truth they fight with each other with weapons of falsehood. In the name of love they conceive hatred for each other. In the name of peace, they declare war upon each other. In the name of compassion, they are motivated by vindictive passion. This inner dichotomy can be dissolved only through direct realization of the non-temporal in which all diversity is unified.

The non-temporal is the abode of undying freshness and freedom. It nourishes the spirit in its ever-fresh greenness. It enables a person to participate in authentic life eternal beyond all permanent fixtures. It lifts one above the false permanence of fixed forms. A hidden tendency of the human mind is to escape from freedom. Freedom has a terrifying aspect. It wears the mask of dread. For those who are not emotionally mature, it rouses unbearable feelings of anxiety and insecurity. It produces a kind of vertigo. So people are usually eager to settle down with a set of fixed ideas. They seek security in some well-established castle of philosophical thinking or religious creed or political ideology. They yearn to hand over the burden of life to some authority figure—to a prophet, messiah, guru, *avatāra*, or benevolent dictator—so that they may live happily ever after. This brings no doubt some peace of mind. But it is the peace of spiritual stagnation. It blocks further growth of personality. It sets in motion the process of decay and degeneration.

The non-temporal reveals the intrinsic value and ultimate significance of individuality. The person who has had a glimpse of the non-temporal is capable of temporarily renouncing the whole world and existing in the medium of his absolute relationship to the absolute. He can go alone in his response to the Alone (*Kevala*). He can take a firm stand in the face of world-wide opposition. And he does so in disregard of personal profit and loss. He does so in a spirit of ego-sacrifice at the altar of cosmic welfare.

In the non-temporal dimension of existence, the individual and the universal meet together in perfect identity or non-difference (*advaita*). This is the significance of the Vedāntic saying: 'Thou art That' or 'I am in essence one with Brahman'. This is also the significance of the saying of the Christ: 'I and my Father in heaven are one.' Christology in its eagerness to give a uniquely exalted position to Jesus has failed to grasp the universal significance of his teaching. In truth his teaching was quite in harmony with the fundamental affirmation of all the great mystics of the world. It centres round the divine heritage of man—his essential rootedness in the non-temporal in which man and God, the individual and the universal, are one. Man has the power within him to contact that unifying ground of existence. Such a contact liberates him from his ego-shell and manifests his latent divinity.

Man's first direct contact with the non-temporal is an overwhelming experience. His entire being appears to be swallowed up in it. All psychic energy is withdrawn from the outside world and the social reality. The delight of the new tremendous discovery inundates his whole existence. In consequence, the outside world appears unreal. The flux of time seems to be a shadow show. One feels the magnetic pull of one transcendent goal—the goal of self-annihilation in the peaceful bosom of the eternal. This is illustrated in the parable of the doll made of salt that went to measure the depth of the ocean. As soon as the salt doll descended into the ocean, it got dissolved there. Who was going to measure what thereafter? The dualism of I and Thou is completely dissolved in the ocean of the non-temporal.

But if the cataclysmic experience of the non-temporal has a chance to mature, in course of time a deeper level of harmony is attained. The content of such experience is gradually assimilated into the concrete texture of human personality. The ecstasy of the eternal ceases to be an exclusive experience. It does not exclude any more the world of space, time and causality. One can be in communication with the outside world and yet be firmly anchored in one's identity with the non-temporal. One looks around, sees mountains and rivers, sky-scrapers and market places, but sees them as they are, in their true proportions, in the background of the eternal. This is what Sri Aurobindo has called 'waking union with the Divine'. Sri Raman Maharshi has called it 'the perfectly natural condition of the self'. The world of space, time and causality appears as a meaningful mode of manifestation of the non-temporal.

Such waking union with the Divine is possible due to some kind of spiritual rebirth of the ego. Like the doll of salt in the ocean, the ego is no doubt dissolved in the depth of the eternal. But it is the ignorant ego, the separative consciousness of the individual, which is thus liquidated. The egocentric individual, who says 'I exist in my solid singleness like a Lucretian atom, separate from fellow-beings and separate from God', receives his burial in the vastness of the infinite upon mystic union with it. But out of the ruins of the ego is resurrected the enlightened I, the cosmo-centric individual, who says 'I am one with the All of existence and with God. All things live, move and have their being in the medium of one all-comprehensive Being'. Such spiritual rebirth is a mode of existence in profound peace, joy, love and harmony. It carries in its heart the vision of the equality of all in the identity of the One.

The immediate awareness of the eternal reaches its height of maturity when it becomes a dynamic and creative force in life. At the preceding stage, one perceives the world as a mode of manifestation of the eternal, and yet may not fully grasp the evolutionary significance of the world-process. One may feel deep compassion for fellow beings, but such compassion may assume an other-worldly form. It may be aimed at the liberation of fellow-beings from the fetters of this world. It may be chiefly oriented either to a supernatural kingdom of heaven or to pure transcendence in its world-negating form. Full participation in the being of the world is out of joint with such an orientation. One perceives the non-temporal in its pure transcendence, not in its creative immanence. Fascinated by the glory of the eternal, one rejects the intrinsic value of time. One fails to notice that the non-temporal is after all one of the dimensions of existence, even though the most fundamental dimension. But time is no less real and no less valuable a dimension of Being.

Integral experience of the fullness of Being is an essential ingredient of mature selfhood or spiritual adulthood. It transforms the mystic into a dynamic and creative personality. A man of integral experience grasps the significance of cosmic evolution in the context of the eternal. He beholds the advance of history as an ever-new challenge to the creative ability of man. He realizes himself as a focal point of evolution, as a unique and active centre of the eternal. So he participates in life's creative adventure towards the fulfilment of the eternal in time. His ontological insight assumes the form of dynamic self-poise in the heart of Being. This is what Śrī Kṛṣṇa had in his mind when he advised his human disciple Arjuna to be serenely united with the Divine and to fight efficiently in the battlefield of life for the sake of truth, justice and righteousness. Kṛṣṇa in the Gita symbolizes the eternal in its relationship to the world-process—in its relationship to the progress of civilization.

We have noted before that out of the liquidation of the ego-centric individuality of the mystic is born his cosmo-centric individuality, his enlightened 'I'. Similarly on the objective side another profound transformation may take place in the due course of maturation of the mystic process. First, in the depth of the eternal the personal and anthropomorphic God of popular religion is liquidated. The ordinary theological conception of God as a jealous, personal, patronizing deity, emotionally tied to a particulat tribe, race, or nation is transcended. The divine 'Thou' of cultural and religious parochialism is buried in the vast immensity of the eternal. But then, out of that burial is resurrected the universal 'Thou' of the evolutionary world-spirit. It is realized that the eternal is not static and world-negating. In the heart of the eternal is an unceasing creative urge perpetually productive of ever-new values. The non-temporal is also the dynamic universal. The eternal has its creative dynamism—its mode of unfettered self-expression in the medium of time. This creative dynamism of the eternal is the evolutionary world-spirit. It is related to man as an eternal Thou, seeking his free and loving co-operation for the production of higher values. Kṛṣṇa in the Gita symbolizes this dynamic divine Thou. Man's highest fulfilment lies in entering into creative fellowship with the universal divine 'Thou'.

THE DYNAMIC UNIVERSAL (ŚAKTI)

We have stressed the point that pure transcendence holds within it an unceasing creative urge. The eternal is also the dynamic universal. In other words, the creative dynamism of time is no less real and valuable than the non-temporal dimension of existence. They are inseparable and interpenetrative aspects of the same Being.

By the dynamic universal we mean the cosmic creative energy (Śakti), or just the cosmic creativity. Western philosophers have variously called it fundamental energy, universal life force, unconscious will, the power drive, cosmic mind, absolute idea, etc. In the light of our previous discussion it may be stated that the universal creative energy must by its very nature be indeterminable. To give it any determinate character is to ignore its universal function. To identify it either with physical energy or with vital impetus or with psychic libido is to limit it to a particular class of phenomena or a determinate set of processes. As soon as such an equation is made, it loses its universal character. Only a dogmatic and reductionistic attitude can affirm a determinate principle to be universal. For instance, a naturalist may hold that physical energy is the key to the world process. In that case he would be obligated to reduce the diversified phenomena of life, mind, spirit and history to the dead level of matter, ignoring their specific character and value. Similarly, an idealist may hold that idea or reason is the key to the world process. In that case he would have to make, as Hegel did, far-fetched efforts to derive natural processes with all their immediacy and contingency from the bloodless categories of abstract logic.

The truth of the matter seems to be that the ultimate creative energy is not to be identified with any determinate logical structure or any particular class of phenomena. Matter, life, mind, spirit, etc. are different levels of manifestation of the alogical dynamic universal. Each order of existence has its distinctive character and value. Every class of phenomena requires a unique set of categories for its proper comprehension. Instead of reducing one class of phenomena to the terms of another, we may bring them all together under the unifying concept of the dynamic universal without abrogating their distinctive features. Instead of explaining one level of existence in terms of another, we may affirm them as different modes of self-expression of the one fundamental creative energy inherent in the eternal.

The concept of the dynamic universal affirms the *reality* of the world process. In ultimate analysis, the world is neither a dream nor an illusion. It is neither an organized subjective experience nor a dispensable objective unreality. It is a real process of change, beginningless and endless. A continuous flux of exciting happenings and challenging events.

But even that is not all. The concept of the dynamic universal also implies an evolutionary perspective of life. The world is a process of emergent evolution. It is a 'perpetual upspringing of ever unforeseen and unforeseeable forms, qualities and values'. The flux of time is constantly bringing to light ever fresh novelties. Unprecedented combinations of events provide occasions for the emergence of new values. Unique life-situations present new opportunities of self-expression. Ever new problems constantly arise to stimulate new creative effort.

Now, the dynamic universal (Śakti) which we have affirmed as an essential aspect or dimension of Being—as the creative dynamism of the non-temporal—may be understood either metaphysically or phenomenologically.

Metaphysically understood, the dynamic universal is a unitary all-embracing creative principle. It need not be conceived as a unitary and unchanging substance. We have already made the point that the category of substance is inapplicable to ultimate reality. The dynamic universal may be interpreted as one indeterminable cosmic dynamism endowed with boundless potentiality. Physical, vital and mental forms of energy are modes of manifestation of that fundamental energy.

Phenomenologically interpreted, the dynamic universal is the totality of all phenomena, observed and observable, past, present and future. It is the experiential whole of all dynamic processes in the world. Cosmic creativity is a convenient conceptual shorthand for all such processes or events.

But from the practical standpoint of yoga, the above controversial issue between metaphysics and phenomenology is irrelevant. A disciplined organization of life towards maximum fruitfulness does not in any way depend upon a prior intellectual solution of this intellectual issue—an issue which is intellectually insoluble.

Whether the world-process be interpreted metaphysically as a unitary force of cosmic evolution or phenomenologically as a flux of phenomena, the fact remains that all manner of creative processes are constantly going on in the world around us. Different atoms combine to form a molecule. Different molecules combine to form the valuable material things we use. Oxygen and hydrogen combine in definite proportions to give rise to water with its new emergent qualities. Carbon, hydrogen, oxygen and nitrogen combine to give birth to a protoplasm with its emergent life-value. The physical, chemical and vital forces operative in the human organism combine to form a constellation which is fit to manifest the radically new emergent quality of self-consciousness.

When in a growing individual the conscious mind and the unconscious psyche, reason and passion, thought and emotion, are harmonized and integrated, the unique emergent value of selfhood is born. The individual actualizes his profoundest potentiality. Then again, people belonging to different tribes, races and religious faiths, combine to form a modern State endowed with its juristic personality and political sovereignty. Historical circumstances further induce different nations to combine to form a unified international organization as an instrument of international peace, justice and harmony. So on and so forth. Cosmic creativity or the dynamic universal signifies all such creative processes and evolutionary achievements. It also signifies all those unpredictable creative events which are yet to be born with the passing of time.

The world-process then presents these three fundamental characteristics. It is a real flux of events, not an unreal dream, nor a senseless shadow-show. Secondly, with its unlimited and multiform fullness, the world breaks through all limiting conceptual formulations. It cannot be equated with any particular thought system, whether scientific, metaphysical or theological. It presents divergent aspects and characteristics which are variously selected, emphasized and interpreted in different thought systems. Thirdly, the world-process reveals boundless creativity. It is an unceasing process of new creation. It is an unfettered drive in the direction of the unseen.

It follows from the above that our understanding of the world is incomplete without an evolutionary perspective. Our understanding of man-in-the-world is incomplete without an historical orientation.

To grasp the meaning of evolution is to participate in it. One who comprehends the creative significance of the world would consider life incomplete without active co-operation with the dynamic world-spirit. There can be no self-perfection without self-identification with the creative force of evolution.

There can be no understanding of man's position in the world without an understanding of the history of civilization. To grasp the meaning of history is to participate in it. There can be no self-perfection in a complete withdrawal from the historical order. Life is incomplete without intelligent co-operation with the creative time-spirit. However profound one's vision of the eternal, it is onesided and imperfect without an active awareness of the eternal and intrinsic significance of time.

THE INDIVIDUAL

The production of endless diversity seems to be the specific business of the cosmic creative energy, of the dynamic universal (Śakti). Individuality is a unique emergent value. There are different grades of actualization of this value.

No two things are absolutely alike in this world. No two trees, not even two leaves of the same tree, are quite identical. No two flowers, nor two fingers of the same hand, are quite identical. Each has a unique texture and configuration of its own. Each has its own distinctive share of the space-time continuum. Each has its own specific relatedness to the cosmic whole.

Man stands out in the animal kingdom with a high-grade individuality potential. Whereas other animals are born as finished types, endowed with unchanging instinctual abilities, man is born unfinished and most helpless. But he is born with the inherent ability to finish an unfinished job. As a fuller image of cosmic creativity, he is born with a task and a responsibility—the task of realizing his hidden possibilities and the responsibility of fashioning his own destiny. His nervous system is the most flexible, so that he may learn and recreate himself with limitless freedom. As the architect of his own fortune, he is constantly surpassing his own 'isness'. He is perpetually reaching out for something higher and greater and nobler. His hopes and aspirations, his drives and dreams, his choosing and rechoosing, are no less vital to his existence than his actuality at a given moment.

The human individual is more or less aware of his freedom and of his dynamic relationship to the world around him. It is a monumental folly to think of the human soul as a self-enclosed spiritual atom or as a static unchanging mental substance. The individual certainly does not exist by himself like a Lucretian atom, solid in singleness. The self-subsistent individual is a mere abstraction of thought. Man grows through constant intercourse with nature and society. The individual derives his physical and spiritual nourishment from them and reacts upon them in his own unique way. Shut out from such active intercourse, he perishes.

There is nothing unchanging about the spiritual substance of the human individual. From hour to hour, from day to day, from year to year, he is undergoing constant change. His beliefs, thoughts, feelings, desires, emotional reactions, etc. are always changing. His attitudes to others—to friends and foes and strangers—are always changing. If he shuts the windows of his life upon all outside changes, he stops growing and becomes ossified. If, on the contrary, he learns to meet all changes from the centre of his own being, he advances along the highway of creative growth. The one thread of continuity that runs through all the changes of his life is his unique pattern of self-development. It is his own pattern of receiving from the world and giving back to the world. It is his unique mode of relatedness to the universe.

There are different essential aspects of man's relationship to the real.

First of all, man is organically and yet creatively related to nature. He is an intelligent tool-making animal. He has the ability to supplement ceaselessly the powers of his body with suitable tools and machines fashioned out of the raw material of nature. He has the power to penetrate to the hidden mysteries of nature and exploit them for his own comfort, happiness and progress. Steamship and railroad, aeroplane and rocket, radio and television, calculating machine and electronic brain, etc. are the marvels of his technological genius. The great danger, however, lies in the possibility of becoming a victim of his own creation. He runs the risk of being crushed by the Frankenstein he has created. He can rise above this risk only by keeping alive in his heart a clear vision of such spiritual values as unity, freedom and love. One has to set aside all techniques and methods of division in order to perceive the indivisible ground of existence. Technology has to be supplemented with the art of silent self-communion in order to prevent man's enslavement by the machine.

Secondly, man is dynamically related to the flux of time. Alfred Korzybski has righly observed that man is a 'time-binding creature'.[1] Man is time-binding because he has the ability to profit from the experiences of the past and ride upon the shoulders of his forefathers. The accumulated wisdom of bygone ages is crystallized in culture and tradition. Via tradition he inherits the riches of the past and creatively advances into the future. He constantly projects himself into the future in terms of his constructive plans of self-development and social progress. The present in which he lives thus embraces both the past and the future. The past is operative in him as habit, disposition and tradition. The future is operative in him as ideal, hope and aspiration. Thus time with all its dimensions becomes the substance of his creative growth.

Man is not only a time-binding creature, but also a time-bound creature. On the one hand he experiences time as creative energy. On the other hand he experiences time as a big question mark. The

[1] Alfred Korzybski, *Science and Sanity* (Pennsylvania: 1941), p. 376.

boundaries of his existence in time oppress him like the walls of a prison-house. He experiences life as an uncertain interval between two unknowns, as a brief flash in a mysterious background of darkness. What happens to him after death is a perpetual mystery. What he was and where he was before death is another intriguing mystery. With his creative imagination he proceeds to fill these mysterious gaps of life with his theories of pre-existence and post-existence. Perhaps his imagination touches a vital chord in the heart of reality. Perhaps his imagination with all its emotional and pragmatic value is out of touch with objective reality. But be that as it may, creative imagination is without doubt an inexhaustible source of new creation in the cultural dimension. The mysterious gaps of life are a perpetual challenge to the spirit in man. Yoga is a radical way of meeting this challenge. Setting aside all theory and imagination, it aims to penetrate to the ground of existence behind life and death with the integrated power of being.

Thirdly, the human individual is inextricably related to society. Interpersonal relations in the social medium are indeed the most vital factor in the structure of human reality. Apart from society the individual is nothing, a mere abstraction. Every individual is born in a particular tribe or community or nation. His growing psyche is shaped and moulded by the cultural forces of the nursing social matrix. One can hardly escape the pervasive and potent influence of socio-cultural conditioning. But with the growth of personality the social horizon of a person may more and more broaden. As different societies and cultural groups come into close contact and interaction, the door is opened to the discovery and appreciation of other races and cultures. One begins to learn to draw upon the cultural heritage of the whole human race. One begins to participate in the growth of civilization in the spirit of a world citizen. One's mental and ethical outlook may be extended even beyond the limits of the human race. There are some rare individuals whose ethical horizon is so broadened that they feel themselves as integral members of the entire living creation, animal as well as human. They experience a sense of responsibility for all life. They are inwardly suffused with universal compassion (*mahākarunā*). They are animated with a spirit of dedication to cosmic welfare. The practice of yoga which involves selfless action and meditation may produce this world-wide expansion of consciousness. When a person is united with the ground of existence, he vividly perceives the oneness of the universe. Luminous vision of the oneness of all produces in turn the spirit of universal love.

In the fourth place, man by virtue of his self-consciousness is dynamically related to his own inmost self. Conscious self-relatedness is indeed the most fundamental imperative of spiritual growth. The transition from tribal to racial consciousness, from racial to national consciousness, from national to international consciousness, and finally from international to cosmic consciousness, can be mediated only by the deepening of individuality. A person who is wholly submerged in the tribal, communal or racial consciousness has not yet discovered his own individuality. He lacks the courage to lift his voice of protest against the senseless conventions and unjust practices of his own group. In order to be able to rise above the limitations of his own group, he has to experience the inward strength and freedom of his individuality. In order to take a bold stand against the hateful conflicts and suicidal wars between different tribes or races, one has to hear the voice of Being in the depth of one's own soul. Likewise it requires the courage and vision of individuality to rise above national and power-bloc differences and take a fearless stand for international justice and peace. It requires the reckless daring of the solitary self to pronounce judgement upon falsehood and hypocrisy wherever he sees them. Critical evaluation and comprehensive vision are the twin functions of mature selfhood. Critical evaluation liberates one from the bonds of parochialism. Comprehensive vision unveils the universal truth which cuts across all geographical, national and religious boundaries.

The individual can become his own true self only by following the inner rhythm of his own being (*swabhava*). He has to discover the law of his own becoming—the law of immanent self-development (*swadharma*). Blind imitation of an external standard is damaging to the growth of individuality. Unthinking conformity to a fixed pattern kills the inner spirit. It makes man a machine. It turns potential genius into a robot. It creates the false glamour of a crow dancing in peacock's feathers. Herein lies the crisis of contemporary man. The danger of the mechanization of life, of automaton conformity, of glittering superficiality, stares him in the face. The danger of anonymous mediocrity moulded by mass media of suggestion and devoured by colossal organizations poses today the greatest threat to the individual when he is right in the midst of celebrating his individuality.

The true self of the human individual is the element of pure transcendence in him. It is the creative spark of the eternal. The more the individual becomes aware of his inmost self, the more he discovers his basic relatedness to the eternal. The more he learns to exist in the medium of his relatedness to the eternal, the more he experiences the strength and freedom of himself as an individual. He realizes that in his essence he is not a mere cog in the machine of a State or a Party or an Institution. He has a mode of existence and self-fulfilment beyond all social groupings and massive organizations. Standing all alone in the presence of the Alone, he discovers the most creative depth of his personality. The clamorous demands of all collectivities—whether state or church or party—are hushed into silence. The ever-tightening bonds of emotional attachment are cut asunder. The claims and counter-claims of conventional morality are submerged in the silent appreciation of the absolute Good.

But there is need for caution even in one's encounter with the eternal. History tells us that man has blundered not only in equating the world of determinate forms with the absolute. He has also blundered in equating the formless and the timeless with the absolute. The latter blunder has produced the spirit of world and life negation. It has encouraged in various forms asceticism, pessimism, supernaturalism, other-worldliness, transcendentalism, etc. Integral philosophy wishes to expose the fallacy of such false equation.

The eternal is certainly the most fundamental dimension of Being. But, as it has already been stressed, the dynamic universal—the creativity of time—is no less real and no less significant an aspect or dimension of Being. The absolute is the eternal-universal (*śiva-śakti*). The eternal is the formless root or the sustaining dimension of the universe. The universal is the creative impetus of the eternal manifesting itself in endless forms in the ever-expanding medium of time.

An integral insight into the structure of the absolute as the eternal-universal gives rise to the most balanced ideal of life. It is the ideal of joyful participation in the creative adventure of life and evolution on the basis of integrated union with the eternal. It is the ideal of creative self-expression, either individually, or socially through some freely chosen institution or organization, in accordance with one's perception of higher values.

CHAPTER VII

SOME METHODS OF MEDITATION

THE essence of integral yoga lies in the balanced union of meditation and action. It is only through such union that creative freedom can be achieved. Through meditation one is more and more integrated with the inner self and united with the supreme Being. Through action one is more and more integrated with the outward environment, natural, social and historical, and communicates with the creative force of evolution.

If a person happens to be an extreme extrovert, meditation would kindle the light of introspective self-awareness which is needed to deepen one's insight into the higher values of life. If a person happens to be an extreme introvert, selfless action would increasingly sharpen his awareness of the reality and significance of the world process. Proper combination of meditation and action in the practice of integral yoga would make a person either an introverted extrovert or an extroverted introvert. Meditation helps in getting rid of emotional conflicts, inner self-discrepancies, and psychic tensions. It is a kind of psychological house-cleaning, a mental catharsis, which knocks out all unconscious obstructions to the full functioning of human personality. Intelligent and selfless action helps in getting rid of all discords and disharmonies in one's relations with the social environment. It clears the ground for constructive co-operation with fellow men in building up a better and nobler human society and in advancing the cause of civilization.

How to meditate properly? What are the most fruitful methods of meditation? Wrong ideas about meditation and misguided practice of it would lead one nowhere and might even be harmful. There are people, for instance, who think that meditation is a kind of mental gymnastic aimed at the eventual annihilation of the mind. Some think of meditation as a kind of reverie or day dreaming, a means of being transported into the realm of phantasy. Some again imagine that meditation is the technique of experiencing strange visions, mysterious sounds, and all manner of unusual bodily sensations. Such distorted notions about meditation often mislead people away from the true spiritual path. Malpractices based upon them serve often as an exciting escape from the stern realities of social existence.

They may open the door to all manner of self-deception and hallucinatory lotus-eating. That is why the need for a competent teacher (guru) has always been considered very essential in the practice of meditation and yoga. Intelligently practised under competent guidance, meditation may tap the vast resources of human personality and immensely contribute to its fullness of growth and creative expression.

THE METHOD OF CONCENTRATION

The most common and traditional method of meditation is that of concentration. It consists in the intelligent focusing of one's attention upon a spiritually significant object or symbol. Popular religion in all countries furnishes people with an abundance of spiritually significant symbols.

In Buddhism, the image of the Buddha, the lotus, the thunderbolt, the wheel, etc. are such symbols. In Christianity the image of the Christ and the cross are the most important symbols. The Star of David in Judaism and the Crescent Moon in Islam, are regarded as significant. In Hinduism the image of Kṛṣṇa or Rāma or some other divine incarnation, the image of Śiva (wisdom), Viṣṇu (love), Kāli (power), or some other representation of the supreme Godhead, the image of Lakṣmī (prosperity), Saraswati (learning and skill), Ganeśa (success), or some other value of life, are very popular symbols. The sacred syllable AUM, and different geometrical diagrams including Śrī Yantra, Swastika, and others, are also considered powerful and highly significant symbols in Hindu religion. According to one's background, faith and choice, one may select any such spiritual symbol from any religion and use it as the focal point of concentration. Increasing attention is to be paid to the inner significance of the symbol which expresses the nature of the truth in some form or other, and stresses the need for reconstructing life in the light of truth. Such concentration may be accompanied by constant utterance, in silence or slightly aloud, of some suitable spiritual formula (*mantram*). By combining verbal symbols with visual images the psychic energy of the individual is channelled in the direction of the spiritual ideal of life. The following are some spiritual formulae which are often used with profit during the practice of concentration:

1. God is all-powerful, all-wise and all-good; may I function as an instrument of the Divine Will.
2. God is the unity of truth, beauty and goodness; may I live as a channel of expression of higher values.
3. God is the unity of wisdom, love and power; I am essentially part and parcel of God.
4. God is the cosmic consciousness in which all creatures live,

move and have their being; may I act as an instrument of cosmic welfare.

5. God is life eternal, cosmic intelligence, and infinite delight (*sat cit ananda*); I am in essence a spark of the Divine.
6. *Aum Brahman, satyam, śivam sundaram.* (Reality is perfect silence and creative logos; it is true, good and beautiful).
7. *Aum Brahman, śāntam śivam advaitam.* (Reality is the unity of being and becoming, time and eternity; it is quiet, harmonious and nondual).
8. *Aum mani padme hūm.* (Truth is the unity of wisdom and love; may I be united with that.)
9. *Aum śānti śānti śānti.* (God is ineffable peace, peace, peace.)
10. *Aum Śrī Hari Aum.* (God is the supreme love and saving grace.)

The regular practice of such audio-visual concentration has the effect of channelling thought energy along the spiritual avenue. It produces a lift in consciousness and inspires one to live in tune with the infinite. When a person has sufficiently advanced in the practice of concentration on concrete symbols, he is in a position to make the transition from the concrete to the abstract, from the symbol to the symbolized. He is now capable of directing attention to the universal truth underlying all determinate symbols. Until this higher transition is made, a person remains more or less in the stage of idolatry, however subtle and disguised that idolatry may be.

The essence of idolatry lies in the identification of the symbol with the symbolized, of the particular with the universal. Such historical figures as Gautam Buddha, Kṛṣṇa, Moses, Zoroaster, Lao-tzu, Jesus Christ, Mohammed, etc. have some divinity or uncommon holiness about them. They may be regarded as particular manifestations in history of the one universal and timeless Godhead. The divine spark which is latent in all was actively manifest in them in an extraordinary degree. But when their followers fail to grasp the self-transcending significance of their Masters as symbols of the one formless Godhead, they become idolatrous. They fasten upon this or that particular religious figure or symbol as exhausting the infinite essence of the Divine. Their idolatrous thinking is manifested in the form of dogmatism, fanaticism and parochialism. A dogmatist exalts his own symbol above all other symbols. For him the symbol is the absolute, the form is the final truth. His idolatrous attitude is expressed in the form of emotional fixation upon a particular historical figure accompanied by denunciation or lack of appreciation of other historical figures. His parochial outlook is reflected in beliefs like: 'Jesus is the only Son of God; Buddha,

Kṛṣṇa, Mohammed, etc. are only enlightened men', 'Mohammed is the last, youngest and therefore most perfect messenger of God', 'Buddha is the essence of all existence; the founders of other religions are at best His different incarnations', 'Kṛṣṇa alone is the completest incarnation of God; others are no more than partial incarnations', and so on and so forth.

The greatest need of our present time is to rise above such parochial thinking, and to develop a cosmic perspective in religion. In the interests of cultural harmony and human unity it is important for us to realize today that the founders of the great historical religions were equally divine and equally human manifestations in history of the one dynamic world-spirit. Each had a particular mission to fulfil in a particular historical epoch. Each delivered a message which was particularly needed at the time. In order to be useful and effective, the teaching of each had to be cast into a mould in conformity with the intellectual climate and socio-political conditions of the time. With changes in human society the mould of teaching or formulation of truth must needs change. Appreciation of the immense value and significance of a particular historical-religious figure need not involve attaching absoluteness and finality to his teaching in all its details.

People with a high degree of intellectual development may practise meditation without the use of any popular image or symbol, whether it be the symbol of a deity like Śiva or Kāli, or the image of an historical figure like Buddha, Christ or Kṛṣṇa, or the image of one's own living guru. They may feel competent enough to contemplate directly the meaning of God as the fundamental spiritual reality of the universe, or as the unity of truth, beauty, goodness and freedom, or as the universal self, etc. Such contemplation would use some abstract and comprehensive idea of God as the basis of meditation. To facilitate an uninterrupted flow of contemplation, the continued use of a suitable spiritual formula or *mantram* would be useful in this connection also.

But even in such a case it must be realized that however profound, comprehensive and philosophically perfect the conception of God may be, it is not to be identified with the reality of God. By means of meditation and in the course of gradual spiritual unfoldment one has finally to transcend, not only sensuous images and concrete symbols, but also abstract ideas, concepts and intellectual formulations, in order to obtain immediate contact with ultimate reality. The philosophical notion of God is no less a symbol than the religious image, even though it may be much subtler and much more refined. Consequently, identification of the concept with the reality is no less idolatrous than that of the image with the reality, even though it may be much more elusive in nature. It is such intellectual idolatry which we find in the absolutistic systems of metaphysicians like Fichte, Schelling and Hegel. The ultimate goal of meditation lies beyond the intellectual as well as beyond the mere sensuous and the mere emotional. Meditation aims at existential contact with pure Transcendence. It is the art of communication with the unfathomable mystery of Being.

It has already been noted that those who feel no need for concrete visual images may still find it helpful to use some suitable spiritual formula (*mantram*) as a support for sustained concentration in the right direction. Meditation is the art of using significant symbols, whether visual, auditory, verbal or conceptual, in such a way that ultimately one should rise above all symbols and directly contact the symbolized reality on a non-verbal level. With the aid of symbols it seeks to transcend all symbols in the direction of the supreme Silence.

COMMUNION WITH NATURE

Nature has always been a deep and unfailing source of inspiration to man. Intimate contact with nature is ennobling and revitalizing. Contemplation of the beauty and sublimity, the majesty and grandeur, of nature, has the effect of lifting man into the sphere of transcendent joy and rapture. It calls forth his deepest creative energies. So a fruitful mode of meditation consists in the contemplation of some particularly fascinating aspect of nature. As you quietly sit down, you visualize nature in one of her soul-entrancing aspects such as the starry heavens above, the boundless ocean below, the majestic grandeur of a mountain, the lovely texture of a flower, the sparkling vivacity of a running stream, the all-consuming power and purity of a flame, and so on. Any one of them may be used as a symbol of the infinite or the cosmic soul or the fundamental creative energy. Or, any such object of nature may be contemplated in its pure suchness or 'is'-ness as an intrinsic value by itself. Through the contemplation of the suchness of a particular object of nature one eventually contacts the ground of all that is. For instance, while contemplating the vast expanse of the ocean, one may gradually lose one's consciousness in it, allowing the spirit of the ocean to penetrate one's being. Thus one becomes one with the ocean. Through the ocean one becomes one with the spirit of nature. Through nature one becomes one with the infinite.

Another approach would be this. While concentrating on the ocean, one may think of it as the symbol of that all-embracing cosmic consciousness that sustains the universe. On the surface of the ocean are the endless roaring billows, but at the depth of the ocean is impenetrable calmness and serenity. Similarly, on the surface of that cosmic consciousness is this world of manifestation—the phenomenal world with all its chance and change, flux and mutation. But at the depth of the cosmic consciousness is the peace that passeth the understanding, the ineffable serenity of the Supreme. Then the meditator may think of himself as a wave on the bosom of that ocean of consciousness; one with it and yet a differentiated entity—a playful individualized form of the ocean.

The same procedure may be followed in the use of other natural symbols. While contemplating a flower, lose your consciousness in it. Allow the reality of the flower to penetrate your soul—the flower as it is in itself, the flower as an outpouring of the soul of nature, the flower in all its beauty of form and strength of individuality. Through such contemplation you enter into the spirit of nature, and through nature you enter into the inmost sanctuary of the absolute spirit. Similarly, in contemplating a mountain, you allow the mountain to express itself through your consciousness. By utmost receptivity and self-opening, conquer the apparent gulf which separates the knower and the knowable. Allow the grandeur and sublimity of the mountain to deliver to your soul its message from the infinite. Or, concentrate upon the mountain as a material image of the absolute. As a sublime image of the absolute, it is at once daunting and fascinating, awe-inspiring and enchanting. On the one hand it mysteriously draws the mind with an irresistable attraction, and on the other hand it makes the mind feel humble beyond measure. It produces a timeless perspective, calling attention to the vanity and stupidity of much of our ordinary living. It inspires one to sublime heights of comprehensive thinking.

CONCENTRATION OF DIFFERENT CENTRES OF CONSCIOUSNESS

The practice of concentration is also possible with reference to different centres of consciousness within the psycho-physical system of man. Corresponding to different levels and powers of consciousness there are different nerve-plexuses and glands in the human organism. This is a significant implication of psycholophysical parallelism. Special stimulation of different nerve-plexuses, glands, and brain cells, accompanies mental functioning of different types and on different levels. The Hindu theory of *cakras*[1] (centres of consciousness) is based upon this fact.

For instance, we have the navel centre (*manipura*, the solar

[1] Arthur Avalon, *The Serpent Power*, 5th ed. (Madras: Ganesh & Co. Ltd., 1953), Chapter V.

plexus) which is regarded as the centre of the larger vital in man.[1] Special stimulation of this centre stirs up higher ambitions and supplies abundant vital energy which may go into the fulfilment of such ends of life as power, position, prosperity, prestige and renown. Then we have the heart centre (*anāhata cakra, hṛdpadma,* cardiac plexus) which is the centre of sublime emotion. Special stimulation of this centre opens the floodgates of love and devotion. Then there is the wisdom centre in the space between the two eye-brows (*ājñā cakra,* the pineal and pituitary glands). Special stimulation of this centre is an accompaniment of what is called the opening of the third eye, i.e. penetrative insight into the meaning of life and the development of the timeless perspective. Then there is the cerebral centre (*sahasrāra,* the thousand-petalled lotus) on the top of the skull, which is regarded as the centre of profound spiritual realization and self-integration. Full activation of this centre is the physiological concomitant of the superb flowering of individuality on the basis of conscious union with the cosmic whole. It is a prelude to the integration of the different aspects of personality, private and social, intellectual and emotional, contemplative and dynamic, introvert and extrovert. So it implies the union of wisdom and love, meditation and action, self-abiding and self-expressing.

A widely practised method of meditation is to concentrate upon the heart centre, visualizing there a lotus or a flame, symbolizing the presence of divine love in the heart of man. At the centre of the lotus or the flame one may visualize one's favourite form of God such as Buddha, Christ, Kṛṣṇa, Śiva, Viṣṇu, Kāli, etc., or one's favourite religious symbol such as the wheel, the cross, the Oṁkāra, the star of David, the crescent moon, etc. Such visualization is usually accompanied by the repetition of a suitable *mantram* affirming the spirit of total and unreserved self-surrender to the Divine.

THE PRACTICE OF JAPAM

A well-tried and time-honoured method of concentration is called *Japam.* It is believed that one can realize God by constant practice of *Japam* alone.

You choose a particular name of God or a certain aspect of the Supreme according to your special liking. Or, perhaps your spiritual guide (*guru*) gives you a suitable spiritual formula on the basis of his insight into your nature, temperament, psychic make-up, stage of inner evolution, etc. The form or aspect of the Divine selected with special reference to the psychic make-up of a particular indi-

[1] Sri Aurobindo, *On Yoga II, Tome One* (Pondicherry: Sri Aurobindo Ashram, 1958), p. 369.

vidual is called that individual's *Iṣṭa Devatā* (chosen deity). It reflects the inner requirement of his soul and embodies the appropriate ideal of his life. It is this chosen deity which is enshrined in the holy word which is given to the individual by his guru. It has the potency of galvanizing the individual into sustained creative effort.

After you receive your *mantram* from a guru, you fix it at the centre of your consciousness, and make it the pivot of your life. You constantly repeat it during meditation with intelligent attention to its deep significance. But that is not all. During the rest of your waking hours also, whatever you may be doing, whether you are walking along the street, or waiting for the bus at the street corner, or riding the elevator in a big department store, constantly affirm the truth and spirit of love embodied in the *mantram*. The more you do so, the more it becomes a dynamic force in your consciousness, a source of strength, inspiration and divine protection against adverse and undivine forces. It gradually builds around you an invisible and impenetrable spiritual armour, proof against the assaults of darkness and evil.

According to an ancient Hindu story, Vālmīki, the celebrated author of the great Hindu epic The Rāmāyana, was in his youth a great sinner, a highway robber, known as Ratnākar. One day he pounced upon an unwary brahmin on a lonely path, and demanded from him whatever money he had. The brahmin stated that he was a very poor man with no more than Rs.2.50 with him as the sole means of subsistence for his whole family for the week. When the robber was about to snatch the money away under the threat of killing, the brahmin reminded him of the wages of sin and of the dire consequence of murder. The robber said that robbery was his means of livelihood. It was also his sole means of maintaining his large family. Consequently, he argued, his action could not be sinful. But in case it was, he had his whole family to share with him the consequence of sin. At that the brahmin said, 'All right, I shall gladly give you this money I have. But first you go to your family and find out whether any one of your near ones was really willing to share responsibility for your sinful action.'

The robber went to his family and interrogated his parents, and his wife and children. That was indeed the bitterest lesson of his life. He found out to his utter disillusionment that he alone was responsible for his actions, and that it was his duty to maintain his family in the best way he could. Neither his wife nor his parents nor his children were willing to accept responsibility for his sin. He was brought to his senses. Thoroughly repentent, he came back to the brahmin, threw himself at the latter's feet, and wanted to know how he could gain liberation from the accumulated sin of his whole past.

The brahmin prescribed for him the holy name of RĀMA, which is a name of God, that must be repeated a ten million times. But unfortunately the robber was such a hardened criminal that he could not even pronounce the sacred name of RĀMA. Now in Sanskrit spelling the reverse of the word RĀMA is MARĀ, which means a corpse, with which the robber was certainly quite familiar through his own murderous actions. At the brahmin's suggestion, as the robber was uttering the word MARĀ repeatedly and fast, he suddenly caught himself at one stage successfully pronouncing RĀMA. With a resolute determination he then took his seat under a large tree and began to perform *Japam* by repeating the holy name of RĀMA until all his sins were washed away. Day after day, month after month, year after year, the robber's uninterrupted concentration on the name of God continued until his whole body was covered in a termite hill. Eventually his sustained flow of meditation resulted in great illumination. Deep spiritual intuition dawned upon his mind. He was blessed with the vision of God as RĀMA. He felt inspiration to write a magnificent epic narrating the world-redeeming activities of RĀMA, the heroic incarnation of God as truth and righteousness. Thus the sinner Ratnāker was transformed through *Japam* into the seer-poet Vālmīki, renowned author of The Rāmāyana.

MECHANICAL AND LOGICAL CONCENTRATION

The above story is an illustration of the value of single-minded concentration as a means to inner illumination. Regular practice of concentration gradually enhances the mind's ability to marshal the normally scattered rays of consciousness in a meaningful way. It is like transforming the mind into a powerful searchlight from an ordinary kerosene lamp or candle flame. Deep powers of penetrative insight into the essence of whatever is brought into the focus of consciousness result from such practice. In the course of meditation the searchlight of the concentrated mind is directed to the ultimate truth, to the meaning of God and the self, and to the significance of life and the world process.

It should be noted here that integral yoga does not encourage concentration in the form of gazing. The act of gazing is an unintelligent, mechanical process. It results in the black-out of rational consciousness, and may produce either sleep or unconscious revery or self-hypnosis. In integral yoga, concentration should be practised only in its intelligent and logical form. The mind should be allowed to play freely around a central theme; thoughts should be allowed to flow unfettered, exploring the different aspects of the theme; there should be no forceful suppression of ideas and feelings, no smothering of disagreeable suggestions, no mechanical straining, no acrobatic exercise, no fighting with oneself. Only, the free functioning of the mind should be accompanied by a genuine concern for the truth and nothing but the truth. Intelligent concentration is in essence meaningful penetration into the heart of the real. It may be likened to the act of shooting an arrow or triggering a gun. The spiritual symbol or the *mantram* used in the practice of concentration is like the bow or the gun. The mind is the arrow or the bullet. Concentration is the act of shooting or triggering. The result is the hitting of the target, that is to say, the experience of oneness with the real.

CONCENTRATION ON THE FLOW OF BREATH

Many people find it particularly easy and immensely rewarding to practise concentration on the flow of their own breath. The constant flow of breath is always there as the most vital fact of one's existence. There is no fear of its running away.

Take your seat quietly in an erect posture, and adopt a relaxed and detached attitude. Then begin to observe with utmost passivity the incoming and outgoing flow of your breath, without any intention of active interference therewith. Just observe it, don't try to change it or control it. In consequence of such observation, the act of breathing may, of course, automatically undergo some alteration now and then. But let there be no conscious effort on your part to effect any kind of change in the process of breathing. After a period of such passive and detached observation, begin to pay attention to the supreme mystery of life as reflected in the simple act of breathing. Without your knowledge or conscious co-operation, the physiological processes of respiration are going on all the time, day and night, during waking and sleep, being controlled and regulated from somewhere within yourself, from the deepest centre of your own existence. It is the miraculous manifestation within the individual of the cosmic life force, the *élan vital*. Through the simple act of breathing, the life force operative within the individual is in constant interaction and dynamic interplay with the universal life force, freely drawing upon that limitless reservoir of energy and throwing out the waste products of its operation. This profound mystery of life would vividly emerge into one's consciousness through quiet contemplation of its physical expression, i.e. breathing. It can be enormously revitalizing.

Another simple form of breathing exercise may be mentioned here. Take your seat in erect posture in a quiet place where there is free play of fresh air. Then take in your breath slowly, very slowly, as slowly as you can, until your chest is filled with fresh air. As you are thus inhaling, think that your whole system is being filled with light, life and love, or with strength, purity and knowledge. Having deeply taken in the full breath, hold it for a while, say for 10–15–20 seconds. While holding the breath, repeat some such *mantram* as '*Aum Brahman*' or '*Aum Śānti Śānti Śānti*' or 'God is light, life and love'. Let the *mantram* reverberate through your entire existence, through all the strata of your being. Then throw out the breath, slowly, very slowly, as slowly as you can. At the time of exhaling, your natural tendency might be to throw out the whole breath at once, abruptly. But you have to practise a little self-control there. While slowly exhaling, think that you are eliminating from your system all impurity, weakness and ignorance, or all lethargy, disease and dullness. Having completely given out the breath, repeat the process ten or twelve times. Gradually you may increase the number of such rounds of breathing and the duration of practice.

There are various forms of breathing exercise and bodily posture described in all standard books on *Haṭhayoga*. People sometimes practise them just for the sake of health, strength, youthfulness and longevity. But in *Haṭhayoga* proper which is a scheme of psycho-physical and spiritual discipline, they are mainly intended as an adequate bodily preparation for higher spiritual activities such as concentration and meditation. The body has to be sufficiently strengthened in order to be able to stand the strain of sustained contemplation and moving experiences. The light of truth, which is an overwhelming experience, cannot be duly assimilated and constructively used by those who are weak in body and mind.

There is, however, a danger inherent in the practice of *Haṭhayoga*. It lies in the tendency to lose sight of the spirit for the sake of the body. Preoccupation with one's own body, the joy of vibrant health, extraordinary control over the physical apparatus, the ability to impress people with remarkable physical feats, etc. begin more and more to hold the attention of a successful *Haṭhayogi*. Whereas the yogi of knowledge or devotion has a tendency to neglect the bodily side of existence under the pressure of deeper intellectual, moral and emotional urges, the *Haṭhayogi* has a tendency to lose sight of higher spiritual values such as critical evaluation, self-sacrifice for cosmic good, etc.

The integral yogi has to strike a balance between these extreme tendencies. He may practise with profit some simple *Haṭhayogic* postures and breathing exercises as a means of strengthening and purifying his nervous system. But he cannot afford to spend too much time and energy on the elaborate practice thereof, as is often done. Nor should he exaggerate their importance as a factor in spiritual growth. He should beware of the danger of yogic exercises assuming a physical, mechanical or egocentric character. Even meditation should be practised in such a way that it affords strength, joy and relaxation, and does not degenerate into a compulsive and mechanical routine affair. Practised in the right spirit it can bring about a gradual expansion of consciousness beyond the limits of one's own individual existence. Its ultimate goal is free and joyful communion with the universal life-force—intimate contact with that world-spirit which is dynamically present in nature and social evolution as well as in one's own self.

CONCENTRATION ON THE ABSTRACT

Those who have already developed their power of concentration with the use of concrete images and symbols may further advance to a higher level of abstraction. They may concentrate on the nature of pure space. Space in its essence is infinite, indivisible and all-encompassing. One cannot think of any limit or boundary to space, because every imagined limit would be a limit *in* space, and would consequently lead beyond itself to further space. Every posited boundary would be essentially self-negating, because beyond that boundary there would be either empty *space* or filled *space* to think of. It cannot be said that infinite space is only the summation of endless finite spaces. For, a summation of finite spaces, however prodigiously large, would nonetheless always be finite. In point of fact, finite spaces are only artificial divisions which we make within one indivisible space.

Similarly, one may concentrate on the category of time. Time is like a beginningless and endless stream. One cannot imagine any absolute beginning or absolute end to the time process. The positing of any boundary to time would be a boundary *in* time, and therefore would be self-negating. One can always think of time before the so-called beginning and after the so-called end. And infinite time cannot surely be conceived as the mere aggregation of finite intervals of time. For, an aggregation of finite times, however large, would nonetheless always be finite. Measured periods of time are in truth only artificial divisions which we make within one indivisible flux of time.

Having reflected upon the essential infinity and indivisibility of space and time, one is now ready to contemplate their relativity and organic interrelatedness. Space is relative to time and time is relative to space. And both space and time are relative to the special circumstances of the observer. Since all objects in space are in constant movement, no point in space is ascertainable and measurable without reference to time and the observer. All day long from dawn till dusk one may be sitting in a small room in San Francisco, and think that one's occupancy of a fixed point in space is obviously unaffected in this case by the passage of time. But an intelligent being observing him from the moon will see how with every passing minute he is changing his position in space, moving fast along with his planet earth. The question of his position in space is then meaningless without reference to a given time and a particular observer.

One can more easily comprehend that time cannot be measured without reference to space. It is common knowledge that significant differences exist between San Francisco time, New York time, Paris time, London time, Moscow time, New Delhi time, Tokyo time, and so on. Time without reference to points in space is just meaningless. Time without reference to the standpoint of the observer is also meaningless. Events which appear simultaneous to one observer may be widely separated in time to an observer located at a different place. For example, to an observer on earth an earthquake and the appearance of a comet in the sky may be perceived as simultaneous events. But an observer in Mars may see the appearance of the comet as an event preceding the earthquake by a good interval.

Thus one is led to the concept of one four-dimensional continuum. Space and time are inseparable aspects of that continuum. The standpoint of the observer is also an essential factor in the structure of the space-time continuum. All empirical existents including the whole choir of heaven and furniture of earth emerge into existence, endure for a while, and then perish within the matrix of the space-time continuum. This perpetual coming into existence, abiding in existence, and passing out of existence, suggest some sustaining creative energy. Both the observer and the observed alike are differentiated moments of this comprehensive creative energy. If we carry our reflection sufficiently deep in this direction we come to realize that the fundamental creative energy—the energy of the space-time continuum—is essentially indefinable. It seems to be limitless and inexhaustible. In the course of cosmic evolution it manifests itself in the modes of matter, life, mind, reason, spirit, etc. Who knows what other unforeseeable emergent values are hidden in the womb of the future?

THE METHOD OF DYNAMIC SELF-OPENING

Another method of meditation is that of dynamic self-opening. The meditator concentrates upon the different elements of his being one after another. He turns the searchlight of his attention to his physical nature, his emotional make-up, his intellectual faculties, his aesthetic urges, his social and moral behaviour pattern, etc. As he concentrates upon the different aspects of his personality, he opens them without reserve to the higher light and power of the Divine.

As the meditator opens the physical side of his being to the higher divine consciousness, the power of the eternal is allowed to enter his physical being, suffuse it with new strength, purge it of its weakness, inertia and ailments, knock out its undesirable habits and mannerisms, and turn it into a fit instrument of the divine will. As he opens his vital or desire-nature to the higher divine consciousness, the light and power of the eternal enters into his vital being, purges it of its selfishness and destructive impulses, knocks out its self-discrepancies and inner conflicts, unites it with the universal life force, and turns it into a channel of activity of the Divine. As he opens the mind to the higher divine consciousness, the light of the eternal is allowed to penetrate to its dark corners, divest it of its fixed ideas and obsessions, open up new vistas and horizons, and turn it more and more into an organ of self-articulation of the supreme truth.

As the meditator opens his emotional nature to the joy and beauty of God, to the master of cosmic dance and celestial music, the divine artist is allowed to play freely upon the strings of his heart and make his whole being vibrate in unison with the cosmic purpose of existence. As he opens his surface personality to the subliminal depths of his being, a new process of transformation is brought into play. He begins to hear a new fruitful dialogue that is started between his rational mind and his non-rational psyche. He begins to hear the voice of Being speaking not only from above but within the inmost centre of his own existence.

Whereas upward self-opening consists in the turning of one's personality to the light and power of the transcendent, the superconscious, inward self-opening consists in the turning of one's conscious being to the inmost centre of the unconscious. Inward self-opening opens the channel of communication with the depths of the unconscious psyche. Upward self-opening opens the channel of communication with the heights of pure transcendence. Total self-opening, upward and inward, effectuates the transformation of personality into an effective centre of the Divine which is both within and above. It is the process of plumbing the depths as well as scaling the heights of one's being.

THE METHOD OF SELF-SURRENDER

Another method of meditation is that of self-surrender or self-offering to the Divine. From the spiritual standpoint, our whole life is in essence an act of self-offering (*yajña*) to the Divine. Whatever we do from dawn till dusk and from dusk till dawn, should be done as an act of self-offering at the altar of the supreme. Whatever the nature of our action, whether we are eating or talking, whether we are engaged in some social activity or political service, whether we are writing a poem or working on a mathematical problem, whether we are singing or dancing or doing a piece of scientific research, whether we are nursing the sick or feeding the hungry, we should perform it all as an act of self-offering to the infinite and for the glory of God.

Meditation may be practised in the spirit of self-offering. And through the practice of meditation the spirit of self-offering gradually permeates one's whole being. As meditation perfects the spirit of self-offering, it has to be applied to all the details of daily living.

As the meditator takes his seat quietly, he says to himself that he is not going to do anything by his own effort. In integral yoga, God is the doer, God is the deed, and God is the goal. The yogi invokes the power of God to do meditation for him. He surrenders his physical existence to the divine will and resolves that his body may not go its own egoistic way any more but function as a channel of expression of the Divine. He surrenders his vital nature to the divine will without any reserve and resolves that his desires and emotions may not run riot any more pulling in different directions, but be self-organized into a powerful instrumentation of cosmic love. He surrenders his mind to the divine light and affirms that dogmatic reasoning and wishful thinking, fixed ideas and preconceived notions, obscuring biases and prejudices, must be relentlessly sacrificed. Cleansed free of all dust of impurity, the mind must be silently receptive to the self-revelation of the supreme.

As different thoughts, desires, feelings, and impulses arise in the mind, the yogi observes them with patience and detachment, and offers them to the Divine with the prayer that they may be transmuted into elements of psychic perfection. As different contents of the unconscious mind including deeply buried memories and long-forgotten desires emerge into the foreground of consciousness, he observes them, analyses them, and then offers them to the Divine, just as a worshipper makes an offering of leaves and flowers at the feet of his deity. There is no secret in one's mind which cannot be disclosed to the Divine. There is no hidden corner of one's psyche which cannot be exposed to the all-seeing eye of God. As the spirit of self-offering is more and more strengthened in the course of the practice of meditation, it can be applied with increasing success to all the detailed activities of life. All efforts and movements, all undertakings and achievements, can thus become modes of self-offering to the supreme Value. That would involve the judicious acceptance in life of such ideas, endeavours, contacts and commitments as are in harmony with the cosmic welfare. That would also involve definite rejection of all those ideas, suggestions, movements and associations, which are detrimental to the cosmic good.

This method of active self-surrender to the Divine is based upon the dynamic conception of human personality. The human individual is essentially an active centre of self-expression of Being. He is not an isolated spiritual atom. Nor is he a mere cell of some social collectivity such as the church, state, political party or business corporation. He is in essence a unique creative centre of the Divine, capable of directly relating himself to cosmic welfare.

THE METHOD OF COSMIC LOVE

Closely related to the method of self-surrender to the Divine is that of cosmic love. It consists in filling the heart with the spirit of oneness with the all of existence, and in sending out good will and love to the four corners of the globe. For those who are habitually self-centred in their thinking and introverted in their disposition, the method of cosmic love is an excellent corrective. For those who are extroverted in their outlook and action, this method is an effective aid to meaningful and constructive self-expansion.

Contemplation of God as love opens the springs of love in the human heart. The meditator now sends forth his love to all living creatures. He sends forth his love to all the peoples, races and nations of the world, who are, one and all, different forms of manifestation of the same universal Godhead. The universal love of God entails that each race, or people or nation has a unique contribution to make towards the fulfilment of His cosmic plan, or towards the all-round progress of civilization.

Finally, the meditator sends forth his love to all individual human beings, friend or foe, akin or alien. While thinking of near and dear ones, he imagines himself as a vehicle of divine love in his dealings with them. Divine love is not coercive but persuasive. It is not aggressive or tyrannical but freely self-giving. It is not possessive or domineering but patiently concerned in the beloved's free growth and welfare. It is not intolerant of others' failings and shortcomings, but understanding of the travail of soul-making. While thinking of foes or foreigners, the meditator remembers that they also dwell with him in the same cosmic Self. The enmity of foes is based upon misunderstanding, misinformation or upon a clash of misconceived interests. The indifference or cruelty of foreigners is occasioned by the lack of contact and fruitful communication. Hatred or hostility is no answer to the situation. It further darkens an already dismal state of affairs. Hatred only confirms the enemy in his antagonism, creates a deplorable vicious circle, and recoils upon the hater as a boomerang. It exudes poisonous fumes affecting the hater and the hated alike. On the contrary, love has the magic power of breaking the vicious circle. It disarms opposition, thaws cold relations, turns apathy into warmth, and converts enmity into friendship.

It is important that the spirit of love which is cultivated in meditation must be applied in daily living and human relations. While walking in the street, one may practise the presence of God in all the people one meets and silently send forth his love to them. While working in the office or factory, one may practise the presence of God in all those whom one contacts from day to day, whether subordinate labourers or superior officers, whether rival colleagues or foreign visitors, and allow his interpersonal relations to be governed by the spirit of love and good will. This does not, of course, mean that a person should not sternly turn down improper demands, or that he should not mete out adequate punishment to those who deserve it. The principle of divine love implies that even in saying 'No' to people, or in fighting against injustice and oppression, the motivating factor will be neither hatred nor vengeance, but the love of truth and justice and genuine concern for the ultimate welfare of all concerned. Love is not sentimentalism, but the sentiment of the good in life. It is passionate regard for the creative possibilities of all life.

The method of cosmic love is based upon the vision of the spiritual unity of all existence. According to the fundamental spiritual intuition of mankind, all determinate forms of existence are significant modes of manifestation of the same creative energy of Being.

CHAPTER VIII

MORE METHODS OF MEDITATION

THE more a person advances in spiritual life the deeper is his self-awareness and the wider his range of interest and human sympathy. Regular practice of meditation sharpens his power of critical evaluation, and helps him to gain a balanced perspective of life. Advanced methods of meditation are calculated to integrate intellect and intuition, combining intensified perception of facts with coherent organization thereof. They harmonize thought and emotion, the ability for detached contemplation of the real and the spirit of joyful participation in the flux of living. They unify different aspects of personality, progressively transforming it into a medium of expression of the creative force of evolution.

In this chapter a few more methods of meditation appropriate to higher stages of self-development will be discussed. These methods can be profitably practised by those who are not afraid of free self-expansion and emancipation from narrow emotional ties.

THE METHOD OF FREE SELF-INQUIRY

One may start meditation with an inquiry into the true nature or identity of the self. Who am I? Whence have I come? Whither am I going? What are the different forces, different impulses and motivations, working in me? Do they all belong to me, or, is there any way of distinguishing between those which are truly mine and those which are not? What is the root and basis of the 'I'-consciousness? The 'I' does not seem to be a static and fixed entity. It is constantly growing, expanding, surpassing itself, arranging and re-arranging its inner contents, and transcending them at will.

The 'I' is the knower, the doer and the enjoyer. It is the centre of its own world which it explores and enjoys, in which it acts and is acted upon. But in order to know itself as the centre of a world, the light of some deeper consciousness is needed. That deeper consciousness transcends the ego-as-related-to-its-world. It is the sustaining medium of the 'I' relating itself in various ways to the universe. Since this deeper consciousness is in essential structure radically different from the objective consciousness of the 'I', it may with some justification be called the Unconscious. It may perhaps better be called the Superconscious.

At first an individual is aware of himself as an object, because he is identified with his body. That is why a child or a primitive refers to himself as 'me'. With the deepening of inner consciousness, the grown-up individual grasps himself as the subject. He now distinguishes himself from the external world as a centre of free action. He also begins to look upon his own body as an object of his 'I'-consciousness. But can he stop there? A free inquiry into the essence of the self opens up profound insights. It is realized that the subject is essentially different from the object. Conversely, whatever can be known as an object is essentially different from the subject. So, following a process of 'not this, not this' (*neti neti*), the subject realizes itself as essentially different from the body, the senses, the mind, the intellect, the soul conceived as a self-contained spiritual substance, and even the unconscious psyche conceived as the opposite pole to the conscious mind. All these can be brought into the focus of consciousness as objective contents of knowledge. Just as the expressions 'my hat', 'my house', etc. reflect the awareness that the self is different from the hat and the house, similarly, such expressions as my body, my mind, my intellect, my soul, my unconscious psyche, etc. reflect the basic realization of the self as the transcendental subject which is not to be identified with any or all of its objective contents.

But at this stage a deeper insight is likely to emerge. Even though the subject is essentially different from the object, it is what it is in inseparable relationship to the object. Subject and object are inextricably related to each other. They are intertwined elements of the same relational situation. This means that the subject in order to be subject has to be known as relative to as well as distinct from the object. Now, who knows the subject? If that which knows the subject is also described as the subject, we would fall into an infinite regress, because the question would endlessly arise, Who knows this other subject? So a deeper truth reveals itself here. That which establishes both the subject and the object in their distinctness and mutual relatedness is pure unobjective consciousness. It is egoless, nonrelational and all-embracing consciousness. It is the basis of the whole subject-object polarization. It is the sustaining medium of the entire relational complex 'I-This' or 'I-Thou'. It is the fundamental spiritual root of the universe. Thus meditation upon 'Who am I' may ultimately guide one into the inmost sanctuary of one infinite cosmic consciousness. But as we said before, such cosmic consciousness may as well be designated the Unconscious, the Superconscious, or Emptiness.

THE METHOD OF DETACHED SELF-OBSERVATION

For those who are spiritually developed enough not to be afraid of their own selves—who are not under any inner compulsion of constantly running away from their inner nature—the method of detached self-observation is very effective and fruitful. In India there is the custom of putting off one's shoes at the door before entering the meditation room. This is not only a precautionary measure against contamination. It carries the symbolical meaning of leaving behind all worries, anxieties and worldly preoccupations prior to the act of meditation. One has to shake off the dust of secular concerns while seeking an audience with the supreme spirit.

Having entered the meditation room, take your seat in erect posture, be quiet, completely relax and let go your mind and body. Give up the idea of having to do something or to engage in any strenuous exercise. The art of doing nothing, just relaxing, is no less important than the capacity for various actions.

A yoga instructor once remarked that meditation was like the art of snake-charming. The charmer brings a snake out of his basket and carefully lets it go. He allows it to play around freely without interfering with its movement. But all the time he keeps a close watch upon it. Similarly, in following the method of detached observation, you are not supposed to concentrate upon anything in particular, nor to control your breath or thought movement, but just to let go your mind and allow it free and full play. The mind is like a serpent which plays around in tortuous ways and has the treacherous habit of bringing up every now and then extremely disturbing thoughts, distracting suggestions, alluring hints and rejected impulses. The mind has also been compared to a monkey, restlessly jumping around and tasting all sorts of fruits from the tree of life. The method of detached observation consists in watching, without being scared, carried off or upset, the serpentine movement or restless jumping-around of the mind. All one's ideas, feelings, desires, impulses, sensations, etc. may be allowed to fly freely across the mental firmament like a flock of birds. One just sits back calmly and watches them in a spirit of non-attachment.

As you carry on meditation in the form of passive self-observation, whether you like it or not, all kinds of changes may be taking place without your deliberately initiating them. Sometimes your mind may be reduced to a mere blank or may drop into a state of vacancy. In that case, detach yourself from that mental condition too, and observe it as an objective content. Sometimes you may find yourself soaring up on the free wings of imagination. In that case, allow the imagination to have its free play, but stand back and watch. Gradually the unconscious mind becomes more and more activated, and in consequence, long-forgotten memories, long-suppressed desires, hitherto-unrecognized impulses, wild expectations, secret longings, deeply buried emotional conflicts and the like, released from the underground prison-house, will keep bubbling up to the surface of the mind. One has to face them all with boldness and unruffled calmness. They may be allowed to emerge freely into the focus of consciousness and unfold themselves without let or hindrance. This provides an opportunity for getting to know one's own nature in its fullness.

In case any undesirable content of the unconscious becomes alarmingly powerful and tends to get fixed in the mind as a compulsive urge, the spiritual guide (guru) has to be consulted. The implication may be that some area of life was unduly excluded from one's consciously adopted scheme of living and striving. In that case there should be a patient broadening of one's plan of living. It may be necessary to set aside for some time the practice of free communication with the unconscious psyche. The practice may be resumed after the neglected area of life has been duly accepted, affirmed and integrated, resulting in greater emotional stability and inward strength. Eventually, there is no doubt that the whole unconscious has got to be explored, understood and integrated with the conscious personality with a view to integral self-fulfilment.

In course of the practice of detached observation it may sometimes happen that a very alluring idea or colourful desire suddenly dashes into the field of vision and carries the meditator off into a realm of phantasy. So he is now transported beyond himself into a wonderland of reverie or day-dreaming, unconsciously identified with an overpowering drive of the unconscious. Sometimes again a very ugly and demonic thought may swiftly surge up to overwhelm him in such a way that he finds himself enchained in a dark dungeon. This happens when he is thrown off his guard and pushed out of his position as a detached onlooker. But as soon as he realizes what has happened, he must resume his position as a detached onlooker, disengage himself from the flux of psychic contents, and remember that the true self is the principle of pure consciousness which is intrinsically and eternally free, free beyond all psychic polarities. Good and evil alike are modifications of the mind-stuff (*citta*) from which the authentic self is to be sharply distinguished.

In the course of his training in the detached observation of whatever comes into the mental field there comes a stage when the meditator gets behind even his own observing ego and acquires transcendental awareness of himself observing the mental flux. At this point, he transcends the subject as well as the object, the 'I' as well as 'this' (*aham* as well as *idam*), and discovers the pure self or spirit of which the subject and the object are two poles of self-expression. Detachment from the mental flux is followed by detachment from even the observing ego, eventually resulting in the realization of the pure self (*puruṣa*) as absolute freedom. In integral yoga it is important to note that the perfect realization of the self as freedom is essentially a dynamic and creative act. The self in its essence is creative freedom. When the meditator transcends the distinction between subject and object, he does not enter into a state of self-annihiliation. On the contrary, he contacts the ultimate source of all existence and perceives that source to be the free creative spirit. Such perception gives him the knowledge and power to reconstruct his whole being as a channel of expression of the supreme. To realize the pure self is not to lose all interest in life. On the contrary one attains thereby that blissful freedom on the basis of which the entire personality is remade in the light of truth and the whole fabric of social relations is reorganized in the spirit of cosmic love.

Habitual practice of self-observation imparts to one's personality the dynamic quality of constantly surpassing oneself. In integral yoga the practice of passive self-observation is carried on within the framework of active self-offering to the divine will. The more the mind is emptied of personal likes and dislikes, of impure thoughts and biased evaluations, the greater is the clarity with which the divine purpose of life is revealed. Thus the practice of self-observation becomes a factor in the transition from unauthentic existence to authentic self-existence. It becomes conducive to unceasing progress —ever reaching out for newer and higher values. It prevents one from getting fossilized or petrified in smug self-complacency on the basis of what has already been achieved. It prevents one from getting into the habit of resting upon the laurels of the past. On the basis of balanced evaluation of what is being achieved from day to day it keeps alive a continuous process of dynamic growth and creative fulfilment, always enlarging the frontiers of one's existence and breaking upon ever new horizons. Moreover, it enables one to cognize oneself from other people's points of view and to evaluate one's performance in different life situations in terms of the reactions of friends and foes alike. This provides an essential basis for increasing self-improvement and for tactful handling of human relations.

THE METHOD OF FREE THINKING

One of the higher forms of meditation is that of free thinking or independent reflection. It consists in increasing the flexibility and mobility of the mind and in acquiring a readiness to follow the wind of truth whithersoever it blows. It consists in cultivating the habit of approaching every subject with an open and unbiased mind, free of predilections and prepossessions. Biases and prejudices, preconceived ideas and temperamental leanings, socio-cultural conditioning imposed by the accident of birth in a particular community, and the like, are among the chief hindrances to the unclouded vision of truth. Free thinking lies in conducting the search for truth from the depth of one's own self. It consists in referring all ideas and beliefs ultimately to one's inner judgement. It presupposes, to be sure, a certain degree of intellectual development. Success in this matter depends upon the ability to pursue an idea to its furthest logical conclusion, undaunted by the opposition of tradition and authority and undisturbed by the possibility of disagreeable practical consequences. In order to be able to embark upon the meditation of free thinking, one must have the courage to sacrifice one's pet beliefs and fixed ideas, selfish interests and emotional crutches, at the altar of truth.

Let me briefly indicate here in concrete terms how one may go about practising this higher form of meditation. The meditator may take up a particular subject such as the meaning of God, the concept of spirit, the notion of immortality, and the like. He approaches the subject with an open mind and concentrates on it in an intelligent manner. As different ideas pour into his mind, he jots them down. As different views emerge from his past studies and discussion, he carefully distinguishes them. He inquires into the logical foundations of these different ideas and viewpoints. Then he refers the whole matter to his own inner self and tries to find out the response of his inner being, however unworthy that response may appear to be. He asks himself the question: 'What seems to *me* to be the truth about the matter on the basis of *my own* experience and in the light of *my own* judgement.' Maybe he has the feeling that his personal experience and intellectual development are too inadequate to justify any worthwhile judgement. But adequate or inadequate, right or wrong, it is important to find out what his own experience, reasoning and unconscious intuition indicate. Because that is of vital importance to him.

The more a person is trained in the art of consulting the inner light of his own mind, the increasingly brighter it shines, producing ever new insights. Setting on one side all hearsay and tradition, he must make an honest effort to feel the pulse of his inner consciousness and to take note of its uninhibited reactions to different ideas about a subject. For at least once he must summon up sufficient courage to say: 'I am not going to accept anything as true simply because Plato has said so, or Saṁkara has said so, or simply on the authority of

Jesus or Gautama. What Plato or Saṁkara or Jesus or Gautama says is perhaps far truer than what my inner self indicates to me. But the judgement of my inner self is of far greater importance to me as the starting point of my further investigation. This is especially so if I am interested in the free and full growth of my own personality or in the complete realization of my own inherent potential. In the meantime, however, for the sake of my own inner stability and for guidance in practical affairs, I may provisionally accept the basic rulings of some such authority as especially appeals to me.'

Suppose now that following this search for the inner light you arrive at a definite conclusion and formulate a determinate view of your own. Don't for heaven's sake make the mistake of making a new dogma out of it and getting attached thereto. The spirit of non-attachment is the essential condition of success in the meditation of unfettered thinking. The results of independent investigation, however broadbased upon logical grounds they might be, should not be regarded as the complete and final truth or as the last word of wisdom. They just furnish you with a spring-board for further adventures in the domain of truth. Since no particular view or theory or conceptual formulation can ever express the whole truth about anything, do not hesitate to confront your own view with other fundamentally opposed viewpoints with patience, sympathy, tolerance and respect. Try to discern with an open mind the elements of truth embedded in other viewpoints. An unbiased and objective survey of conflicting views and reviews, yours and theirs, is sure to be richly rewarding. It is conducive to the attainment of higher and higher levels of understanding. The meditation of unfettered reflection moves forward dialectically to unsuspected vistas of the infinitely manifold truth.

You may start with a great book of wisdom like the Upaniṣads, the Gītā, the Bible, the Dhammapada, the Talmud, the Koran, the Zend Avesta, the Book of Changes, etc. Or, you may start with the recorded insights of any such great master as Plato, Saṁkara, Lao-tze, Spinoza, Emerson, Schweitzer, Ramkrishna, Aurobindo, Gandhi, etc. Read a little and then think about it. Try to grasp its full significance, its manifold implications, and its bearings upon life. Try to find out what appears to you to be the true meaning of what you have read, and whether or how far it differs from other interpretations of the same that you know of. It may also be that you feel unable with all humility to accept in toto what you have read. If so, frankly and boldly face the fact. Try to find out on what grounds you cannot accept this or that passage of the book. This may indicate a significant new angle to the whole subject matter, suggesting a new line of interpretation or critical evaluation. It may also, to be sure, indicate that there is a need for greater experience and training on your part for proper comprehension of the matter. In any event it is a fruitful way of carrying on contemplation—unfettered contemplation in fearless pursuit of the truth. It enables one to feel the pulse of one's own inner consciousness. It is also helpful in unfolding the perspective of life particularly relevant to one's own growth of personality.

Free thinking is the basis of creative self-expression. As the thinker pursues an idea to its furthest logical conclusions, as he refers different ideas to his inner self and takes note of his spontaneous reactions, as he makes an unbiased survey of different conflicting viewpoints including his own, he prepares himself for creative insight. He jots down the various ideas that emerge into consciousness. He may then proceed to organize them in a logical sequence and develop them into an aesthetic whole of self-expression. In the course of such self-expression, fresh ideas are likely to crop up, new vistas of thought may open, important changes and modifications may suggest themselves. As he presses forward in this enterprise of free self-articulation, creative endeavour becomes more and more penetrative and productive. Free creation becomes at the same time unimpeded self-explication of the real. Meditation takes on the form of the self-utterance of reality itself. As an individual thinks, reality thinks itself out through him.

MEDITATION AS SPIRITUALLY ORIENTED ACTION

It has already been stated that meditation, rightly understood, is not the negation of action, but rather the basis of intelligent and efficient action. Meditation and action are like the inhaling and exhaling, or like the systole and diastole, of spiritual life. Meditation is the act of self-knowing; action is that of self-giving. Meditation aims at inner illumination; action is the outflow of compassion that springs from illumination.

At the beginning, meditation and action appear to be separate processes, each in need of being supplemented by the other. But with the advancement of spiritual life, meditation becomes more and more dynamic and creative, and action becomes more and more meditative or spiritually oriented. In integral yoga meditation has to be conducted from the very beginning in such a way that one may not fly off at a tangent beyond the realities of the world of action, ending in static self-realization. Likewise, the active side of life has to be organized and oriented from the very outset in such a way that it may not go the way of increasing self-estrangement. Even the most trivial and humdrum activities of social existence may be performed in such a spirit that they assume the form of joyful meditation in action. A brief consideration of the distinctive features of spiritually oriented action—that is to say, of meditation in action—would not be out of place here.

First of all, the spiritual orientation of action involves the application of the principle of concentration in the practical sphere. Concentrate upon the spiritual destiny of life, namely, that of functioning as an instrument of the divine will, that is to say, as an instrument of truth and justice and love and peace. Organize all the various activities of your life around this central ideal. Let the basic spiritual motivation transform all the details of living into significant elements of a self-coherent and meaningful whole. No important aspect of life is to be excluded from this goal-oriented self-organization. Eating, drinking, sleeping, going to parties, choosing the vocation of life and place of residence, selecting the life-mate and circle of friends, etc.—all of these without exception can be made to contribute to the fulfilment of the central purpose of existence.

Try to understand the dynamic potentialities of your nature and the distinctive line of your self-development. In other words, try to find out whether by nature, temperament and aptitude, you are likely to shine most as an engineer or a mechanic, as a doctor or a nurse, as a teacher or a social worker, as a poet or a musician, as a scientist or a philosopher, as a businessman or an office clerk, as a farmer or a factory labourer, and so on and so forth. Having set the goal, bend your energies to the attainment of the goal. Cultivate your latent qualities and acquire proficiency in your chosen field. And then make an offering of yourself—of the best in you—at the altar of cosmic welfare. In other words, look upon your profession not only as a means of serving your personal interest, but also as a medium of serving your country, and through the country, humanity, and through humanity, the will of God. Avoid such circumstances and associations as may distract you from the spiritual ideal of life. Try to create more and more such circumstances and life situations as would be most favourable to your spiritual growth and self-expansion.

Secondly, spiritually oriented action implies the application of the principle of self-observation in the practical sphere. Make a habit of observing yourself in the different situations of life, taking note of how you react emotionally in changing circumstances and in dealings with different people including friends and foes, relatives and strangers. This habit of self-observation has the effect of more and more perfecting one's actions and one's responses to environmental changes. It is an essential factor in the gradual transcendence of one's shortcomings and angularities, idiosyncrasy and emotional immaturity, parochialism and dogmatism. The principle of self-observation is of paramount importance in achieving self-perfection on the one hand and harmony in human relations on the other. There are people who seem to be completely incapable of such self-observation. They are habitually busy projecting their own faults on to other people and blaming their failures and frustrations either on next-door neighbours or on remote stars. The growing ability for objective self-awareness and constructive evaluation of one's own personality is an invaluable aid to gradual self-perfection.

Thirdly, action itself takes on the form of meditation when it is performed as a mode of self-offering to the Divine. From the spiritual standpoint, it is not so much what you do as the spirit in which you do it which is of basic importance. Whatever your profession or avocation in life, if you perform all actions for the glory of God or for the good of humanity and God's creation, your actions become an integral part of spiritual discipline. Through such actions selflessly offered at the altar of the Divine, you increasingly approximate to blissful union with the Divine. Dedication to cosmic welfare is the way of participation in the cosmic adventure of God.

For a spiritual seeker no action is too low or derogatory, not even that of a scavenger or a shoe-shiner. Every man is great in his own position, regardless of his calling or social status. Every occupation carries a dignity of its own in so far as it is a contribution to the joy of living. The underlying spirit of self-offering to the Divine adds a spiritual dimension to its social importance. The more we perform our actions in the consciousness of an instrument of the divine will, the more they become instrumental to our immediate union with the infinite.

Finally, spiritually oriented action is free and spontaneous action, relaxed and non-attached. The more we select our actions in accordance with the chosen ideal of life, and the more that chosen ideal is in harmony with the latent possibilities and aspirations of our inmost self, the more we have a sense of freedom and joy in performing them. That does not mean that we have to avoid completely those actions which are unpleasant and disagreeable. In every sphere of activity, however congenial, one has to take care of certain initially boring details, certain mechanical and routine affairs, which are not quite agreeable at the beginning. But as we learn to view them in relationship to the central ideal or in the context of the total scheme of self-fulfilment, they become increasingly agreeable and pleasant. Steadfast devotion to a well-chosen ideal of life releases the latent energies of the soul. It turns the whole arena of active life into a medium of joyful self-expansion.

The spiritual orientation enables a person to perform the various duties of life in a relaxed attitude. Even in the midst of a full flood of activity, he can maintain his self-poise and peace of mind. Because his central motivation is derived not from any ego drive but from the spirit of dedication to the Divine. He acts not for the aggrandisement of his own little self, but for the glory of God. He acts not for his personal power, position, name and fame, but as an instrument of the divine will. He knows that his work ultimately belongs to God, and therefore it has to be viewed in the context of the eternal. The enduring value of whatever is accomplished would be attributable to the divine power working through his agency. Its continued importance would depend upon the basic requirement of evolution. So there can be no occasion for pride, vanity or elation. If, in the contrary case, his lifetime endeavour falls short of the ideal and counts as a failure, even so there is no need for depression and despair. Because there is no total waste or loss of spiritual values. They are eternally conserved as dynamic forces in the scheme of evolution. Every noble effort, sincerely made, goes to strengthen the process of cosmic evolution, even though it may fail in its immediate objective. Every virtuous action, regardless of outward consequences, contributes to the enrichment and enlargement of one's inner being.

Vanity is indeed out of place in the spiritual frame of orientation. It is good to remember that nobody is absolutely indispensable to any social undertaking. No particular individual, however high and mighty, however gifted and masterly, has a veto power over the march of civilization. There is after all a higher invisible power which is actively concerned in the ongoing of the universe. An insight into the dynamic presence of the Divine in the historical order produces a relaxed attitude without diminishing the spirit of enthusiasm. It enables a person to keep alive in his mind the cosmic vision of truth and justice. It enables him to serve humanity without any illusion of permanence or delusion of grandeur. Spiritual understanding begets the right spirit of non-attachment. It begets non-attachment to the vicissitudes of success and failure, adversity and prosperity, blandishment and vituperation. It also produces non-attachment to the various modes of manifestation of the ego. One plays one's role according to one's highest ideal and to the best of one's ability, and leaves the rest unto the hands of God. All worries and anxieties which stem from lack of the cosmic perspective are consumed in the flame of selfless love. One feels free to function with perfect self-poise as an active playmate of the Divine in the drama of life.

THE INTEGRAL APPROACH

The integral approach in meditation stresses the need for the growth of inner consciousness in preference to rigid conformity to any fixed method or technique. The inner attitude is far more important than outward form. The flexibility, open-mindedness and multi-directional alertness of the mind are far more important than fixed reliance upon any credal support, doctrinal apparatus, elaborate exercise or routine practice. According to the changing needs of the growing psyche one may profitably employ different methods. But the dominating outlook is that of creative fellowship with the evolving world-spirit.

Inherent in the integral approach is the basic ideal of fulfilling life in all its aspects. So integral meditation must assume the form of comprehensive training in both inward integration and outward adjustment. Inwardly, one has more and more to develop the consciousness of being an instrument of the Divine or of cosmic welfare. One has to concentrate on the constructive development of one's latent possibilities in order to perfect one's entire nature as an instument of higher values. One has to strengthen and fulfill all the aspects of one's personality including the physical, the intellectual, the moral, the emotional and the numinous in order to achieve balanced self-unfoldment. Outwardly, one has to acquire increasing insight into the realities of the outside world. One has to know how sharply conflicting forces—good and evil, justice and crime, love and hatred, peace and war—are intertwined in the social fabric. One has to appreciate the value and significance of the different aspects of civilization including the socio-economical, the political, the ethico-religious, the cultural, etc. One has to learn how to play one's role constructively on the stage of social evolution, maintaining self-poise in the vicissitudes of fortune, contributing one's best in a selfless spirit, and turning all circumstances, whether favourable or unfavourable, into stepping-stones to greater fulfilment. In accordance with this concept of total psycho-social adjustment, a daily schedule of meditation, particularly helpful to the beginner, may be outlined as follows:

Start your day in a positive, dynamic and spiritual frame of mind. Before plunging into the daily round of activities, practise meditation for a while, even if just for ten or fifteen minutes. First of all, read a few pages from an authentic book of spiritual wisdom and inspiration. Read and re-read them with an open mind. Carefully reflect upon their significance and their practical bearing upon life and human relations. Then take your seat relaxedly in erect posture and concentrate upon the meaning of God as the dynamic world-spirit or as the unity of higher values. Or, concentrate upon such supreme values as truth, freedom, cosmic welfare, creative action, the progress of civilization, and the like. Reflect upon yourself as an integral part and also a unique and dynamic centre of the world-spirit. The world-spirit is the Divine dynamically present in the world process. Fix in your consciousness the idea of being essentially an instrument of the Divine.

Then make a mental survey of all the important activities and contacts which you propose to go through during the day. Rehearse within yourself how best you want them done. Visualize yourself performing them in the most appropriate way in accordance with the spiritual ideal of life. Don't allow your daily schedule to be overcrowded. Carefully select matters of prior importance, just enough for the day, setting aside other things for the next day. Just as first things have to be done first, right here and now, it is also good to remember that there is always a tomorrow for so many other things to be done, if God so wills. Make a habit of performing those actions which have been intelligently selected in the attitude of serving the Divine. The divine will is indeed the meeting ground of the best interests of one's own self and those of society. Having mentally surveyed the important items of the day's programme and having suffused them with the right attitude, you are now ready to embark upon your daily round of duties.

In the course of the day, whenever you get a little free time, reaffirm in your mind the spiritual ideal of life and rededicate yourself as an instrument of the Divine. This is necessary to prevent one's getting lost in the forest of means and details losing sight of the ultimate end of existence. Repeat in your mind the name of God or some suitable spiritual formula (*mantra*). The more you repeat a significant *mantra*, the more it gathers momentum and becomes powerful in your life, offering you divine protection against dangers and dark forces and keeping alive your sense of direction in life. Intelligent repetition of the *mantra* endows a great idea with creative force, attunes one's whole being to the Divine, and releases the creative energies of the soul.

Finally, before retiring at night, it is a good habit to practise a little meditation, even if it be for ten or fifteen minutes. This time again, first of all, read a few passages from an authentic book of spiritual illumination. Reflect upon their inner significance and practical bearing. Then make a comprehensive and critical review of all the activities, events, experiences and contacts of the day. Regarding some of them you may feel reasonably proud. Offer thanks to God for your good luck or satisfactory performance. Such a spirit of thanksgiving would prevent pride and vanity from running riot. On the contrary, they would be a source of encouragement for further progress. Remembrance of God transmutes egotism into self-confidence and self-esteem.

With regard to some other happenings or activities of the day, you may feel sorry or repentant or depressed. But don't allow such feelings to sour your soul. Analyse the relevant happenings and find out what mistakes were made, what could have been done to avert the unpleasant, what lessons were conveyed through disappointment, and so on and so forth. In the light of such self-analysis and objective understanding of the day's happenings you would be in a position to refashion your future programme of action and tutor yourself in more successful ways of living. Having extracted lessons of the day, brush aside all further thoughts and feelings from the mind. Adopt a completely relaxed attitude and try to establish perfect silence within. Whatever ideas and emotions may pop up, offer them to the Divine with the prayer that your whole being may enter into silent and fruitful communion with the supreme. With this prayerful attitude fixed at the centre of your consciousness, place yourself in the peaceful embrace of sleep.

METHODS OF MEDITATION IN ZEN BUDDHISM

Under the influence of Buddhism, two important schools of meditation (*ch'an* or *zen*) developed in China. One is the Northern Gradual School of Shen-hsiu. The other is the Southern Abrupt School of Hui-neng.

According to the Northern School, meditation is a gradual process of self-unfoldment; *dhyāna* (meditation) gradually leads to *prajñā* (intuitive wisdom). Sustained intellectual effort, moral discipline, spiritual practice, ethical action, etc. are important factors in the attainment of enlightenment. This viewpoint particularly appeals to the intellectual and ethical types of people. The method of meditation conceived here is that of the 'dust-wiping' type. So long as our mind, which is like a mirror, is full of the dust of impure desires and impulses, it does not fully and faithfully reflect the light of truth. Meditation consists in gradually wiping the dust of the mental mirror through concentration upon spiritual truths and regulation of the affairs of life in accordance with the spiritual ideal. The sun of spiritual illumination shines out when the clouds of ignorance and the mists of desire are cleared away from the mental firmament. Thus meditation may be defined as a gradual process of transition, by means of disciplined effort, from bondage to freedom, from ignorance to knowledge, from mediate mental cognition to immediate spiritual realization.

The Southern Abrupt School of Hui-neng is the latest form of development of Zen Buddhism. It maintains that the difference between ignorance and knowledge is a radical and fundamental difference. Spiritual insight (*satori*) is a qualitatively different dimension of experience. There are no degrees of spiritual insight. Either a person has it, or he does not have it. Until a person has attained insight, there is only the process of groping in the dark or the spectacle of self-defeating effort, which cannot be truly called meditation at all. Meditation (*dhyāna*) is in essence inseparable from spiritual intuition or wisdom (*satori* or *prajñā*). Intuition flares up like a flash of lightning, abruptly and mysteriously. There is no way of controlling its appearance in the life of an individual. It is certainly not the consequence or effect of a gradual and continuous process of growth. Since it is qualitatively and dimensionally different from all mental states and processes, it can hardly be conceived as the terminus of a mental process. It is in that sense 'no-mind' or 'no-thought' or just the Unconscious. Spiritual insight or *satori* may suddenly appear when the mind is absolutely relaxed and free from all effort and preoccupation. The dawning of *satori* is like the effortless and spontaneous blooming of the flower, or the shining of the sun, or the singing of the bird.

According to the Southern School then meditation is not a gradual process but a sudden and abrupt leap from mind to no-mind, from darkness to a flash of lightning, from *vikalpa* (the sanskrit word for discursive thinking) to *prajñā* (ontological insight or realization of truth), from *mayoyi* to *satori* (Japanese), from *mi* to *wu* (Chinese). This leap is at once psychological, logical and dialectical. It is not the result of reasoning, but takes place when logical reasoning or dialectical argument has been abandoned as futile and incapable of producing ultimate insight. Psychologically, spiritual intuition flashes forth when the individual's own effort or will power is brought to a finish. This sudden awakening of spiritual intuition may be occasioned in different ways. It may arise through living contact with some illuminated person or guru. It may result from relaxed self-opening to the spirit of nature or the course of history. Zen masters are noted for their employment of different methods of shock treatment. When a disciple approaches the master with the question, 'What is the meaning of Buddha-nature?', the master may reply unexpectedly with a sharp slap on his face or a stunning blow on his head. By some unknown mechanism of the spirit, this may produce sudden enlightenment. A shock treatment like this has the effect of jolting the disciple out of his normal intellectual bent into a deeper level of non-discursive insight. When a disciple approaches the master with the question, 'How long would it take to attain *nirvāṇa*?' the master may reply with the counter-question, 'Did you wash your rice bowl this morning?' The master is here trying to bring the disciple's mind from the clouds of abstract and impersonal speculation down to the concrete events and activities of his own life and indicate that true wisdom would spring from one's whole-hearted participation in the dynamic flow of the living present.

The Southern School believes in the 'self-seeing' type of meditation as distinguished from the dust-wiping type. Meditation is not any strenuous striving for a fixed form or a determinate psychical condition. It is rather the art of non-clinging and letting-alone—the art of allowing things to develop. In traditional theory, the wiping of the dust of impure desires from the mental apparatus is an essential condition of spiritual illumination. But according to Zen in its extreme form, meditation is a sudden and revolutionary leap beyond the mental into the heart of *satori*. The self of man is the light of truth that shines in him. It is the spiritual dimension of his existence. It is intrinsically pure and self-revealing. In consequence, it cannot be defiled by any dust or impurity, just as the sunlight cannot be stained by any external contamination. Purity and brightness are inherent in the self, and therefore cannot be lost to it. Moreover, in the self's spiritual intuition, subject and object, knower and knowable, beholder and visible, etc. become one. In the traditional practice of meditation, ordinary dualistic experience is repeated in the form of introspection. A person's objective perception of the table outside of him is a dualistic experience of himself as knower and of the table as the object of knowledge. When he introspectively observes his own mental states and processes, the latter dualistically appear to him as the objective contents of a transcendental consciousness. In introspection the mind divides itself into two parts: a knower and a knowable. This is prejudicial to the attainment of that identity-consciousness or non-dualistic experience which is the fundamental spiritual reality.

In spiritual wisdom, being appears not as separate from seeing, not as an objective content of subjective apprehension, but as inseparably identical with seeing and experiencing. And this seeing which is being is also acting. It is the flux of life itself, the creative advance of the spirit. The equation 'seeing = being = acting' expresses the essence of the self-seeing type of meditation. It is free and spontaneous living in harmony with the Unconscious, like the blooming of the flower or the shining of the sun or the singing of the bird. In this non-duality of effortless living things appear as they are to the non-discriminating eye of spiritual intuition. When we deliberately differentiate or discriminate, the power of spiritual discernment is lost. For instance, when we discriminate against members of other races and religious faiths, the distinctive qualities of different races and religions are not properly appreciated. We perceive the endless variety of existence in their true colours and proportions when we allow the light of consciousness to shine without any bias, prejudice or discrimination. The true power of discrimination is based upon non-discriminating *prajñā*',[1] just as the non-discriminating light of the sun reveals all things in their distinctive forms. Meditation is the functioning of this 'contentless mirror-nature or self-nature'.[2] It is the attainment of formlessness or emptiness (*śūnyatā*). It is the act of abiding in the Unconscious which is non-abiding in any fixed form or idea or condition.

In traditional practice, meditation is conscious striving for a determinate form of psychic experience or a fixed value. But Zen meditation is non-clinging to any fixed form; it is non-abiding in any specific condition. It is the act of comprehending the Unconscious in day-to-day living and in the flux of daily occurrences. The word Unconscious is used in Zen in a sense profoundly different from that in western psychology. It is not the dark background and basis of the conscious mind. Nor is it a kind of world-spirit floating on the surface of chaos at the time of creation. By the Unconscious is meant the attitude of having thoughts and yet not having them, or the spirit of non-attachment in all the changing conditions of life. 'The Unconscious means to have no-mind in all circumstances, that is to say, not to be determined by any conditions, not to have any affections or hankerings. To face all objective conditions, and yet to be eternally free from any form of stirring, this is the Unconscious.'[3] It is not to think of being and non-being, not to think of good and evil, not to think of enlightening or being enlightened. The Unconscious is to 'let thy will be done', and not to assert one's own. 'All the doings and happenings, including thoughts and feelings which I have or which come to me, are of the divine will as long as there are on my part no clingings, no hankerings.'[4] This is the Unconscious. Meditation (*dhyāna* or *zen*) which is the same as spiritual understanding (*prajñā*) is the awakening of consciousness in the Unconscious.

Now, the question may arise, Is not abiding in the Unconscious a form of clinging? Is not dwelling in one's self-nature a new mode of attachment? This question or doubt springs from a failure to grasp the true meaning behind the outward form of language. The Unconscious or the self-nature is not to be equated with any fixed form, mental condition, psychic process or bodily action. Abiding in the Unconscious means non-abiding in any passing mental condition or process. Dwelling in one's own self-nature means non-clinging to any fixed form or value. These are various modes of expression for complete spiritual freedom dynamically interpreted.

[1] D. T. Suzuki, *Zen Buddhism*, William Barret, ed. (New York: Doubleday Anchor Books, 1956), p. 183.
[2] Ibid, op. cit., p. 183.
[3] Ibid., pp. 192–3.
[4] Ibid, p. 200.

GRADUAL AND ABRUPT SCHOOLS RECONCILED

From the standpoint of Integral Yoga there is no essential incompatibility between the two apparently conflicting schools of Zen Buddhism. Seeming contradiction is due to the imperfection of human language on the one hand and the distorting action of the human mind on the other. It is true that the Northern School of Shen-hsiu encourages conscious striving for enlightenment (*prajñā* or *satori*). It is also true that many seekers after truth have a tendency to misconstrue the self-shiningness of the self as a particular mental state alongside of other mental states and processes. But rightly understood, enlightenment, *nirvāṇa* or *prajñā* is that pure non-temporal consciousness (or the Unconscious) which is essentially different from the flux of successive mental states and processes. As non-temporal awareness, it is not to be visualized as a future psychic event. It is indeed the goal of spiritual seeking, and yet it is not the goal in so far as it is the eternal present of non-temporal awareness. Whereas the Northern School emphasizes it as the ultimate goal, the Southern School stresses its nature as no-goal. From the standpoint of Integral Yoga it may be stated that the non-temporal dimension of existence is at once a future event and an eternal now —a goal and a no-goal. From the practical side of our spiritual quest, realization of the non-temporal is the basic objective. But viewed from the ultimate standpoint of essential truth, the non-temporal is the ever-present reality.

Let us try to express the matter in another way. Supreme enlightenment has two aspects: non-temporal and temporal, non-mental and mental. In the former aspect, enlightenment implies the eternal light of truth, the timeless dimension of existence, the intrinsic luminosity of the self. Understood in this sense, spiritual intuition proper is no-goal, no-mind, no-thought, no-being. But in its temporal aspect, enlightenment means the light of truth as reflected on the purified mind of a particular individual. It is the mystery of being as revealed to an integrated person. It is the intrinsic luminosity of the self as directly apprehended by a spiritual seeker. In this sense, enlightenment is the sought-for goal of an individual. It is that which gives meaning and direction to his life.

The Northern School stresses the need for conscious striving and for the discipline of meditation. The Southern School believes in the futility of conscious effort, the importance of 'absolute passivity dynamically interpreted',[1] and the spontaneity of illumined living. In the scheme of Integral Yoga, there is room for both conscious

[1] Ibid., op. cit., p. 200.

effort rightly oriented and passive self-opening to the sovereign light of truth.

To abandon all conscious striving in the form of morality, religion and other cultural disciplines may induce one to regress or relapse into the animal, primitive or infantile way of living. Since nature abhors vacuum, the discarding of all goal-oriented effort would bring about an upsurge of unconscious instinctual forces, sweeping away the treasures of the centuries of man's cultural development. On the other hand, there is, of course, the human tendency to overdo his ethical or religious role, to push his conscious striving for perfection to undesirable lengths at the prompting of a tyrannical super-ego. In that case, as the Southern School points out, moral and religious efforts become self-defeating. Our best virtues are indeed those which are performed in an unconscious way, so that the left hand does not know what the right hand does. Our deepest wisdom is that which flows unconsciously from a supra-mental source. Conscious individual effort cannot be said to *produce* salvation or liberation. Because in that case, what is produced would be another psychic event or effect in time, another passing mental condition, and not that non-temporal awareness which liberation truly is. Yet conscious discipline has undoubtedly great value within proper limits. Guided in the right direction, it brings the unconscious process of self-integration inherent in all living beings to a higher conscious level and thereby speeds up the tempo of progress. It removes obstacles and impediments from the path of dawning self-realization. It knocks out from one's nature inertia, obtuseness, one-sided tendencies, emotional conflicts, and the like. It is a conscious aid to the unconscious shining out of the light of truth, just as the conscious act of gardening is a great help in the unconscious blossoming of flowers and the ripening of fruits in the garden.

Integral Yoga is the balanced scheme of self-unfoldment in which conscious discipline and unconscious growth are harmoniously fused. Active self-energizing (*tapas*) has to be supplemented by the spirit of passive self-offering (*samarpaṇa*). The effort of self-development has to be geared to the purpose of Being active in the unconscious psyche. The striving of the individual must be re-inforced by the favourable cosmic wind—the grace of God. In order to secure the latter, one has to develop more and more the spirit of total self-giving to the divine will or the cosmic purpose of existence. Self-discipline serves to remove the mists of egocentricity and the clouds of ignorance so that the sunlight of truth may shine out. Divine grace is manifested in the blossoming of love that sheds lustre on life.

Let us now turn to the question: Is meditation a gradual and continuous process of spiritual growth? Or, is it a discrete and abrupt act of illumination?

According to Integral Yoga, the answer to the above question would depend upon the point of view one adopts. The view that spiritual insight is an abrupt and discrete realization stresses the point that it is a radically different dimension of experience and that its attainment involves a revolutionary leap from the ordinary analytical way of thinking (*vikalpa*). The view that meditation is a gradual and continuous process stresses the point that the revolutionary saltus involved in the attainment of spiritual intuition is the culminating point of prolonged inner unfoldment. A disciple meets a master, and something suddenly happens to him. He catches a glimpse of the higher realm of value, or gains a new insight into the meaning of life. This depends on the one hand on the communicative power of the master, and on the other hand on the readiness and receptivity of the disciple who must have been going through a long period of conscious or unconscious self-preparation. It is his readiness to receive the truth which brings him in dynamic and open-minded contact with the master. Many other people who come to see the same master may not experience anything similarly significant happening to them.

Even though the gaining of a fresh insight is abrupt and discrete, it presupposes a long period of silent self-preparation. It also requires a subsequent period of quiet assimilation in order to become a dynamic factor in life and a constructive force in society. For Integral Yoga it is not enough that one attains a new spiritual insight or a profound inner experience. The new insight has to be properly co-ordinated with other areas of human experience so that it may become an effective element in balanced self-fulfilment and in all-round social progress.

Spiritual insight is not a fixed item of knowledge given once and for all. There are different levels of spiritual insight and ever new horizons of truth-vision. There is always room for endless progression in the domain of knowledge. On the spiritual path there is no dead stop which one can proclaim as the last word of wisdom. Meditation as the quest of truth is surely a process of continuous growth and self-unfoldment. It is the process of ceaseless seeing into the infinite richness of truth. It is the process of ever new formulation of the eternal truth in the ever-changing circumstances of life, society and history. In the course of the maturing of personality, there are critical phases representing revolutionary moments of fresh insight. After a new insight is gained, it affects previous knowledge and is also affected by the latter in respect of its precise mode of expression. It has to wait for adequate assimilation, proper evaluation, and meaningful co-ordination with other areas of experience, before it can enter into the flux of life as a stable ingredient thereof. Meditation is thus a gradual process of spiritual evolution with revolutionary phases of new spiritual intuition and new life-transformation.

In view of the fact that different individuals belong to different psychological types and stand at different stages of evolution, Integral Yoga does not altogether discard the traditional methods of meditation. The ancient methods and techniques can be suitably modified and intelligently re-oriented in accordance with the concept of integral and dynamic union with the life-spirit. Integral Yoga advocates the judicious and constructive use of different methods in the case of different individuals, gradually guiding them to the ultimate goal of creative self-fulfilment.

For instance, let us consider the traditional method of passive and detached inward observation of one's own flux of psychic contents. Integral Yoga would not reject this as a static and dualistic mode of practice. This method has great value and potentiality. It is immensely helpful in bringing to light inner tensions and conflicts, and in producing an increasing insight into the inner workings of one's own mind. It is also helpful in gaining the right perspective regarding the thoughts, feelings, impulses, and aspirations of oneself. Some amount of quiet detachment is essential for adequate evaluation of one's inner motivations and emotional reactions to reality, just as active participation in life is essential for the amplitude of experience and acquaintance with the world.

True, detached self-observation involves the polarization of the self into subject and object. And is not such polarization obviously contrary to the spiritual goal of identity-consciousness? Does it not introduce a division into the indivisible unity of life? Yes, it does. But it is by doing so that the essential structure of life as creative unity—not as blank, featureless, static unity—is brought to light. It should be noted here that the object of meditation is not to regress to the primitive consciousness prior to the individual's reflective self-discovery. It does not aim at the infantile 'presentation continuum' or 'tribal participation mystique', which antedated the emergence of reason, conscience and individuality. The true object of meditation is to grasp the supreme mystery of existence in which all kinds of differences arise out of the creative unity of life. Meditation as detached self-observation is an excellent training in understanding how dualities develop within the indivisible unity of being. It helps us to comprehend the polarization of the observing mind and the observed mind as a mode of manifestation of the same creative principle. Integral Yoga employs this method in such a way that ultimately an individual comes to realize his true self as a principle of creative unity which transcends all dualities and at the same time develops them and abides in them. Meditation is not a process of introversion, but a method of dynamic apprehension of the creative spirit in man. It is not a process of regression, but a means of comprehending differences as creative expressions of the One. On the basis of such comprehension, one learns to participate in the various activities of life and yet maintain one's inner self-poise and freedom. One actively engages in creating ever new forms and values and yet refuses to cling to any one of them.

Before concluding it might be worth while restating that the essence of Integral Yoga consists in the union of meditation and action. Through action one descends into the flux of becoming, and partakes of the joys and sorrows of life along with others. Through meditation one contemplates the nature of pure being, gains a broader perspective of becoming, and beholds life in the context of the eternal. Meditation imparts depth, significance, and serenity to the life of action. Action has to release the creative energies of meditation in the sphere of social progress. In the practice of Integral Yoga, action and meditation gradually become fused into one, so that one can actively play one's role in the evolutionary advance of life, without losing the perspective of the eternal. This is non-action in action, moving and yet not moving. Herein lies the secret of enjoying freedom in the innumerable bonds of life. Herein lies the clue to joyful participation in life's festival of light, colour and form.

Through action one effectuates desirable changes in the environment, and creates new values. Through meditation one maintains inner freedom, and prevents petrification in any fixed form or value. Meditation is thus the free-flowing life of creative action. By liberating action from rigid routine and blind conformity, it opens up ever new horizons. By virtue of its communication with the eternal, meditation perpetually revitalizes action to ever new creative urges. When a perfect balance between meditation and action is established, action becomes creative freedom, meditation becomes dynamic knowledge, and life becomes an adventure of meaningful self-expression.

INDEX

Absolute, the, 57, 61, 66, 71, 78, 93–4, 98, 100–4, 106, 116, 119, 122
Absurd, the, 70, 103
Adam, 33
Advaita (non-difference), 106, 119
Aham (the ego), 138
Ahiṁsā (non-violence), 15, 24, 55
Anāsakti (non-attachment), 34
Anaximander, 100
Aparigraha (non-greed, non-acceptance of unnecessary gifts), 24, 55
Archetypal images, 83
Arjuna (chief disciple of the lord Kṛṣṇa), 48–9, 98, 108
Āsana (yogic posture), 53, 55
Ascetic, 37, 39, 40, 42, 49, 60, 66
Asceticism, 48–9, 59, 60–1, 66, 79, 116
Aspiration, 89, 90
Asteya (non-stealing), 24, 55
Ātman (Self), 15, 19, 20–1, 25, 29, 34, 86
AUM (most sacred syllable of the Hindu-Buddhist tradition, symbolizing the Supreme), 118–19, 127
Aurobindo, Sri, 15–16, 31 fn., 41, 48 fn., 107, 123 fn., 140
Avalon, Arthur, 122
Avatāra (incarnation of God), 68, 106
Avidyā (primal ignorance or nescience), 40, 94

Being, 13–17, 19, 25, 27, 31–43, 47, 57, 61–2, 64–5, 71–2, 76–7, 81, 83, 88–9, 102–5, 107–10, 115–17, 121, 130, 132–3, 152
Bernard, Theos, 53 fn.
Beyond good and evil, 24
Bhagavadgītā, the, 14, 37, 47–9, 98, 108–9, 140
Bhakti (devotion), 67, 76
Bhaktiyoga, 39, 66–73
Bhattacharyya, H. D., 40 fn.
Bhāva (emotional attitude), 68–9
Bible, the, 140
Bodhi (spiritual intuition or enlightenment), 72, 96, 103
Bodhisattva (a spiritually enlightened person) 44–5
Book of Changes, the, 140
Brahmacarya (self-discipline), 24, 55
Brahman (Supreme Being), 14, 16, 19, 34–5, 64, 86, 106, 119, 127
Brahman-laya (absorption in the Supreme), 40
Brahmavaivarta Purāna, 40
Brāhmi sthiti (self-poise in Being), 31
Bṛhaspati, 40, 48
Buddha, the, 17, 25, 44–5, 118–20, 123, 148
Buddhism, 43–4, 47, 96, 118, 147, 151
Buddhist, 23, 45, 72

Cakras (centres of consciousness), 122–3
Ch'an (Chinese word for meditation), 147
China, 147
Christ, 25, 35, 45–6, 69, 106, 118, 120, 123
Christian, 23, 33, 39, 43, 69, 72, 96
Christianity, 45–7, 118
Christology, 70, 106
Citta (mind-stuff), 137
Civilization, 16, 28, 76, 81–2, 102, 108, 111, 114, 117, 132, 144–5
Coomaraswamy, Ananda K., 47 fn.
Cosmic consciousness, 72, 96, 115, 119, 121–2, 135
Cosmic creativity, 32–3, 72, 109–12
Cosmic evolution, 51, 57, 59, 97–8, 108, 129, 144
Cosmic love, 25, 31, 98, 131–3, 138
Cosmic man, 23, 33
Cosmic purpose, 38, 43, 76, 91, 95, 130, 152
Cosmic reality, 72, 93–6
Creative adventure, 16, 43, 78, 108, 116
Creative freedom, 14, 16–17, 30, 150
Creative energy, 16, 57, 72–3, 109–10, 112–13, 121, 129, 133
Creative evolution, 15

Dama (restraint), 63
Dayananda, Swami, 14
Das Gupta, S. B., 44 fn.
Dāsya (spirit of service), 67
Devil, the, 60, 79–80, 97
Dhammapada, the, 140
Dharma (law, righteousness, religion, truth), 47